STEP INTO MY KITCHEN
THROUGH THE YEAR

by Evelyn Curtis

First published in 2001 by Evelyn Curtis

ISBN 0-9539806-1-8

Watercolour Illustrations by Rachel Childs
© Oil paintings by Jill De'ath

Cover Photograph by
Mr. Les Curtis,
Curtis & Lane, Sudbury, Suffolk

Designed and printed by
The Lavenham Press, Lavenham, Suffolk CO10 9RN

I dedicate this book to my daughter, Belinda,
who made every day special while she was growing up,
and still does!

Acknowledgements

Writing a cookbook is rather like learning to ride a bike, you don't forget what you have learnt! But here the similarity ends. A writer needs encouragement, and for this, my thanks go to family and friends, especially to my husband who acted as my unpaid chauffeur and chief taster of my recipes during the last 12 months. As a book grows, so does the author's association with the many people involved in its production, and my thanks go to Rachel Childs for her meticulous attention to detail in the beautiful pictures she painted to illustrate each chapter, and to Jill De'ath who loaned her two brilliant and striking oil paintings for my book. My thanks also go to Nellie Smith, who so readily helped me with the baking used on the cover of this book, so that it could be photographed and produced in time, and not least, to The Lavenham Press Printing Team, who saw me through my third cookery book with the same patience, humour and understanding, with special thanks to Amanda Webber for her co-operation and enthusiasm at all times. My thanks to you all.

Evelyn Curtis.

Introduction

My last book was built around people and food, but this book is about food in season, giving seasonal recipes month by month. I've tried to include dishes suited to a particular season, for instance you won't find a thick nourishing soup in the middle of June, when we may be in the middle of a heat wave, instead you'll find strawberries and all the soft fruits that start to arrive as our summer begins. In January there are warming casseroles and soups, made from cheap fresh root vegetables, and hot hearty puddings and pies served with creamy custard and sauces. And, as I think there's no better place to be on a cold winter's day than in my warm kitchen having a baking session with my Aga, you'll find recipes for plenty of cakes, fruit loaves, scones and biscuits, you can try out and bake to your heart's content.

In April and May we begin to see the fresh young vegetables making their appearance on market stalls and shops, with spinach and spring onions and, if we're lucky, sprouting broccoli, and a variety of salads and imported tomatoes, and if we keep a keen eye open, we may see the first of the outdoor grown rhubarb, which should become more plentiful in May.

In June we have the start of the luscious strawberry season, which has been known to carry on right until the end of September to the beginning of October in the strawberry fields of Draycott in Somerset, which is where I saw them, nestling under their dewy green leaves, when I was down there this year. And as the summer months progress English cherries are on the market, and in July gooseberries get plumper and riper, and its not long before we can eat the delicious red eating ones, as well as imported peaches.

As the months pass, we finally come to autumn and winter, and although November brings the shorter and darker evenings, and cold weather, there are compensations with the start of the planning and preparation for December and Christmas, although it's a wonder we have time to cook with all that Christmas entails. But in these two months you will find recipes for soups and puddings and some real comfort food, bringing us into December with all the traditional dishes to plan, including stuffings and trimmings to accompany the roast turkey.

Now that I have given you a *'taste of what to expect'* in my book, I hope you will find your *'step into my kitchen an enjoyable journey through the year'*, as much as I've enjoyed writing about it. *Bon appetit.*

Evelyn Curtis.

Painted by Jill De'at

Contents

Contents – January

January

This month is the start of what I call "winter proper", and usually heralds a long spell of cold weather. It's the time for steaming soups, made from cheap fresh root vegetables, and hot hearty fruit pies and puddings served with sweet, warm sauces.

Seasonal fruits are all citrus, and traditionally winter is the time for making marmalades when the bitter Seville oranges arrive. Early rhubarb comes in this month, and poaching the delicate pink stalks in sugar with a little water is delicious to eat on its own for dessert. My kitchen is filled with the aroma of cooking and baking at this time of the year, and it's definitely the best place to be on the dark cold days of January with the reassuring warmth coming from my Aga.

CREAM OF MUSHROOM SOUP

This is a good well-flavoured soup, which I make throughout the year, and to make it extra low in calories you can leave out the cream. It reheats well and can be frozen for up to one month, otherwise it tends to lose its flavour, but remember to leave out the cream when freezing it.

Serves 4.

Ingredients:

225g (8oz) mushrooms
50g (2oz) butter
600ml (1 pint) chicken stock
Salt & pepper

1 small onion, peeled & chopped
2 dessertspoons arrowroot
425ml (¾ pint) milk
Single cream

Chop mushrooms very finely. Melt the butter in a large saucepan and gently fry the onions, taking care not to let them brown. Then set aside onions, and slowly fry mushrooms in remaining butter, stirring all the time to stop them browning. Then gradually add the stock and milk and onions to the saucepan and simmer on a very low heat for 20 minutes. Meanwhile mix the arrowroot with 2 dessertspoons of water and add to the soup and, stirring continuously, bring the soup to simmering point again, and then simmer for 2 minutes. Season to taste and serve piping hot.

BEAN AND VEGETABLE SOUP

This is one of my favourite soups, and I love the smell of the chopped vegetables and bacon wafting through my kitchen on a cold winter's day, as it simmers away on the Aga hotplate.

Serves 4-6.

Ingredients:

2 carrots, scraped & sliced
2 garlic cloves, crushed
1 small cabbage, shredded
2 celery stalks, sliced
1.5 litres (2½ pints) water
1 teaspoon salt
450g (1lb) dried white haricot beans,
  soaked overnight & drained

6 medium potatoes, peeled & quartered
2 medium onions, peeled & thinly sliced
110g (4oz) streaky bacon, in one piece
1 bouquet garni (thyme, sage & basil)
2 tablespoons parsley, dried or freshly
  chopped

Put beans in a saucepan and cover with water. Bring to the boil and simmer on hot plate for 1 to 1½ hours until the beans are tender. Halfway through the beans' cooking time, put the remaining ingredients in another saucepan. Bring to the boil, then simmer for 30 to 45 minutes, or until the bacon and vegetables are cooked and tender. Remove the bacon and chop it finely. Return to the pan. Discard the bouquet garni. Drain the beans and add to the soup, stirring well. Cook for a further 3 minutes, sprinkle the parsley over the soup, and serve piping hot with crusty bread.

MINESTRONE

This soup has a real Italian flavour, with the pasta making it substantial enough to serve as a meal on its own.

Serves 6.

Ingredients:

1 onion, chopped
2 cloves garlic
1 small turnip, peeled & chopped
1 small leek, chopped
25g (1oz) lean bacon, chopped
25g (1oz) butter
Salt & pepper
1.2 litres (2 pints) beef stock
  (or beef cubes)

2 carrots, scraped & finely chopped
2 sticks celery, chopped
2 large tomatoes, skinned
150g (5oz) green cabbage, shredded
50g (2oz) macaroni
1 glass red wine
Parmesan cheese

Heat butter in large heavy based saucepan, add all vegetables and fry gently for 10 minutes until they soften. Add bacon, garlic and hot stock. Bring to the boil, cover pan and simmer for 15 minutes until vegetables are tender. Add tomatoes and red wine to pan and bring back to the boil. Add pasta and simmer uncovered on low heat for 10-15 minutes. Season to taste, stir a little of the Parmesan cheese into the soup and serve the rest separately.

SPLIT PEA SOUP WITH HAM AND CARROTS

This recipe was given to me by an Australian friend, and I think of it as a real winter soup – I call it 'my plan ahead soup', as the peas have to be soaked overnight. I usually serve it with wholemeal bread.

Serves 4-6.

Ingredients:

350g (12oz) split peas, soaked
  overnight for about 12 hours
1 medium onion, peeled & chopped
A little olive oil
Salt & freshly ground black pepper

2 carrots, scraped, & diced
110g (4oz) ham
1 teaspoon cumin powder
1.5 litres (2½ pints) cold water
1 bay leaf

Soak split peas overnight, or for about 12 hours. Heat a little oil in a saucepan and lightly fry onion and carrots, then sprinkle on the cumin powder. Add split peas, herbs and cold water, and bring to the boil. Cook for about 25 minutes or until peas are tender. Season with salt. Trim fat from ham and cut ham into small strips. Blend half the soup to a purée, and then return soup to the saucepan. Bring to the boil, season with pepper and, just before serving, add ham.

LAMB AND BEAN STEW

January is the month for casseroles and stews to ward off those winter chills. This dish can be prepared the day before cooking. It freezes well too.

Serves 4-6.

Ingredients:

1kg (2¼lb) best end of neck of lamb	50g (2oz) lentils
25g (1oz) haricot beans	25g (1oz) pearl barley
2 large potatoes	1 large turnip
4 carrots	3 onions
2 bay leaves	Salt & black pepper
Bouquet garni	

Soak lentils, haricot beans and pearl barley overnight in cold water. The following day peel and chop all the vegetables and put them into a large saucepan. Trim any excess fat from the best neck end of lamb and cut into single chops. Add lamb, together with bay leaves, salt, pepper and herbs to the vegetables. Drain lentils, haricot beans and pearl barley, and add to the pan. Pour over 2 litres (3½ pints) water, cover the pan with lid and bring to the boil. Simmer gently for 3½ hours. I usually thicken with a little cornflour before spooning into a serving dish.

BRAISED OXTAIL

Oxtail is inclined to be a fatty meat, but if cooked one or two days before it is going to be eaten, so that the fat can settle and be lifted, then it's one of the most nourishing and inexpensive winter meals to ward off January's cold east winds that whip through the Suffolk village I live in like a sharp knife.

Serves 6.

Ingredients:

2 oxtails	35g (1½ozs) beef dripping
1 large onion	2 small turnips
350g (12oz) carrots	Bouquet garni
2 Bay leaves	Salt and pepper
1 tablespoon lemon juice	1 bottle red wine or beef stock cube made up to 600ml (1 pint)

Cut up oxtail and coat in flour. Melt dripping in large pan and fry oxtails for about 5 minutes, and then set aside in a large fireproof casserole. Fry onions in dripping left in pan and then add to oxtails. Pour wine or beef stock over oxtails and bring to the boil. Add salt, pepper, bay leaves and bouquet garni for 1½ - 2 hours. Then strain off the liquid into a large bowl and leave to cool, lift off as much fat as you can, and pour remaining liquid over oxtail. Add peeled and sliced carrots and turnips to oxtail, also add lemon juice, bring to the boil, then cover and simmer in preheated oven 140C, 275F, Gas Mark 1 for 2 hours. Then add peeled tomatoes and simmer for a further 25 minutes. Serve in the casserole in which the oxtail was cooked, no further vegetables are needed, as you can mop up the juices with chunks of crusty bread, or make some dumplings and add to casserole during the last 25 minutes of cooking.

BEEF CASSEROLE

I cook mostly in my Aga, especially in the winter when it really comes into its own, and my electric oven stands forlornly neglected until the summer months arrive. Casseroles are the easiest of meals to prepare and cook, and when all the ingredients are ready, I just add to the meat and liquid, pop it into the Aga's simmering oven and forget all about it until it's needed. But not everyone has an Aga, and the recipes in this book give instructions for cooking by electricity or gas, but cooked slowly your casserole will taste delicious and the meat will be lovely and tender.

Serves 4-6.

Ingredients:

1kg (2¼ lb) lean steak, chuck or
   rump, cubed
175g (6oz) large mushrooms, sliced
300ml (½ pint) beef cube stock
Bouquet garni of parsley, bay leaf
   & thyme

3 medium onions
175g (6oz) button mushrooms
300ml (½ pint) red wine
Salt & black pepper

Peel and slice onions, and fry gently in a little heated oil. Remove and set aside. Add remainder of olive oil to pan, and when really hot, add cubed steak and fry quickly for 2-3 minutes until meat is thoroughly sealed. Add onions to steak, season with pepper and salt, and sprinkle over flour, stirring over a low heat until flour is cooked. Add half the mushrooms and the bouquet garni together with the wine and beef stock. Cover and cook slowly in preheated oven 140C, 275F, Gas Mark 1 for 2½ hours, until meat is tender. Half an hour before the end of the cooking time, add small whole button mushrooms. Remove bouquet garni and serve with creamed potatoes and broccoli.

RABBIT AND BACON PIE

Rabbit is so much easier to come by these days, and most supermarkets stock them jointed and packaged ready for use.

Serves 4.

Ingredients:

1 large rabbit, cleaned & jointed
225g (8oz) streaky bacon,
   trimmed & chopped
2 large onions, peeled & sliced
1 large carrot, scraped &
   roughly chopped

850ml (1½ pints) beef cube stock
2 sticks celery
1 bay leaf
2 tablespoons vegetable oil

Coat the cleaned and jointed rabbit in seasoned flour. Heat oil in heavy based pan and fry joints quickly to seal the juices. Transfer to casserole dish. Lightly soften prepared vegetables in pan with juices and stir in 1 tablespoon flour, and add thyme and sage. Remove from heat and add stock and wine, stirring to remove any lumps. Pour over rabbit in casserole, cover and braise in preheated oven 170C, 325F. Gas Mark 3 for 1½ - 2 hours, until tender. This makes a nice Sunday lunch served with baked potatoes, cabbage and carrots.

HERRINGS FRIED IN OATMEAL

I must admit I do try to grill most foods if they aren't cooked in the oven, but I do make an exception when cooking herrings. I think they are best cooked in a frying pan to give that crispy crunchy outside, and they don't have to be oozing in oil or fat if you drain them thoroughly. In winter they make a welcome change from the usual bacon and eggs for breakfast, or a tasty supper dish garnished with wedges of lemon and plenty of hot buttered toast.

Serves 4.

Ingredients:

4 medium herrings
4 tablespoons fairly coarse oatmeal

3 tablespoons oil
Salt & pepper

Wash, scale and clean herrings, cut off heads and remove backbones (if you ask, your fishmonger will do this for you). Sprinkle insides with salt and pepper, close together and coat thoroughly with oatmeal. Heat oil in frying pan and fry the herrings for about 10 - 15 minutes on each side over a fairly low heat. Serve as above.

APPLE AND CELERY SALAD

This salad is ideal to serve in the winter for lunch or supper with cold meats, and it makes a light starter to a heavy main meal.

Serves 4.

Ingredients:

1 head of celery
1 small onion
3 tablespoons mayonnaise

2 red and 2 green dessert apples
2 tablespoons French dressing
75g (3oz) walnuts, shelled

Wash and finely chop the celery sticks. Peel onion and thinly slice. Wipe the apples, quarter and thinly slice. Mix apple and celery with French dressing, and fold in mayonnaise. Set aside in refrigerator. Before serving, coarsely chop the walnuts and stir them into the apple and celery. Spoon salad into a serving dish and garnish with sprigs of watercress.

PARSNIP PATTIES

In the Somerset village where I grew up, it was always said that parsnips tasted better when "a little frost had nipped them", but you may have your own thoughts on this! I like to eat them roasted with a joint of meat, and I often make these little patties in a batch and freeze them, so that I have some in reserve for when needed.

Serves 4-6.

Ingredients:

1 kg (2¼lb) parsnips, peeled
1 teaspoon black pepper
Fresh brown or white breadcrumbs
Oil or fat for frying

1 tablespoon salt
50g (2oz) butter
1 egg, beaten

Cut the parsnips into thin slices. Bring a pan of water to the boil, add salt and parsnips and simmer for about 25 minutes until parsnips are tender, but not too soft. Drain and cool, then rub parsnips through a fine sieve and beat in butter, salt and pepper. Shape into round patties about 6 cm (2½ inches dia.) Then roll each patty in the breadcrumbs and coat with egg. Leave in refrigerator for about an hour. Heat oil or fat in a deep frying pan and fry quickly on each side. Drain and serve as a second vegetable or as a supper dish with a poached egg or grated cheese on top.

STICKY TOFFEE PUDDING

This warm sticky pudding is just right for a cold January day. I usually make one large pudding, but you can make individual ones, using small dariole dishes, and these ingredients will make roughly 6 to 8 puddings, depending on the size of your darioles. This pudding freezes well and can be re-heated.

Serves 6-8.

Ingredients:

50g (2oz) softened butter, or
   soft margarine
1 large egg, beaten
1 teaspoon baking powder
300ml (½ pint) boiling water
1 teaspoon vanilla essence
75g (3oz) margarine

175g (6oz) caster sugar
225g (8oz) plain flour
175g (6oz) dates, chopped
1 teaspoon bicarbonate of soda
150g (5oz) brown sugar
4 tablespoons double cream

Put dates in boiling water to soak. Beat butter or margarine together with caster sugar and add beaten egg. Add flour and baking powder and mix well. Mix bicarbonate and vanilla into dates, and add to flour mixture. Mix well to make a fairly slack texture. Place in a 1½ litre (2 pint) ovenproof dish and bake in preheated oven 190C, 375F, Gas Mark 5 for 55 to 60 minutes. **To make toffee coating:** Mix together brown sugar, margarine and double cream and bring to the boil in a small saucepan, then simmer for 5 minutes. Pour over the cooked pudding and serve.

TREACLE AND MARMARLADE TART

This is a variation on the traditional treacle tart, with the lemon marmalade giving a sharp tangy taste, and a chance to use up any stale bread you may have.

Serves 6.

Ingredients:

225g (8oz) short crust pastry
110g (4oz) lemon marmalade
2 tablespoons lemon juice

6 tablespoon golden syrup
225g (8oz) white breadcrumbs

Roll out pastry on floured surface and line a greased 20.5cm (8 inch) flan dish. Trim edges and set aside remaining pastry. Warm syrup and marmalade over a very low heat. Remove from heat and stir in breadcrumbs and lemon juice. Pour mixture into pastry case, and then make a lattice pattern made from remaining pastry, thinly rolled out. Bake in preheated hot oven 200C, 400F, Mark 6 until pastry is golden brown. Serve hot or cold.

APRICOT LAYER PUDDING

I've used apricots in this pudding, but you can use the many different varieties of dried fruit available in our shops and supermarkets, and further on in this book you will see a similar recipe, using the season's fresh fruits, in fact I'm tempted to call this recipe "Layer Pudding Of Your Choice"!

Serves 4-6.

Ingredients:
110g (4oz) soft margarine
110g (4oz) caster sugar
2 medium eggs
175g (6oz) self-raising flour
½ tsp baking powder

Filling:
2 small eating apples, peeled & cored
3 tablespoons apricot jam
1 tablespoon lemon juice
75g (3oz) 'No-soak' dried apricots,
    finely chopped

Put all the sponge ingredients into a food processor and mix for about 25 seconds, or put into a large mixing bowl and beat vigorously until nice and creamy. Grease an 850ml (1½ pint) pudding basin. Mix together all the filling ingredients, and then place a layer of the sponge mixture into the base of the pudding basin, and a layer of the fruit mixture. Continue in this way, using alternative layers and finishing with a layer of the sponge mixture. Cover with a circle of greaseproof paper, and use another circle of kitchen foil to cover and seal the pudding. Steam for about 2½ hours. Remove cover and turn out pudding on to a warmed serving dish. Serve hot with homemade custard.

CIDER AND FRUIT CAKE

This cake disappears very quickly in my family, but if you have some left in your cake tin and find it's a bit stale, then cut into thin slices, and buttered it still tastes delicious with a hint of cider.

Ingredients:
175g (6oz) wholemeal self-raising flour
175g (6oz) hard butter or margarine
Rind and half the juice of 1 lemon
180ml (6fl oz) to 225ml (8 fl oz) dry cider
175g (6oz) self-raising flour
175g (6oz) soft light brown sugar
2 tablespoons thick cut marmalade
175g (6oz) mixed dried fruit

Rub butter or margarine into flour until it resembles breadcrumbs. Add the sugar and lemon rind and mix well, then add marmalade and fruit, mixing thoroughly. Add lemon juice and cider until mixture is a soft consistency. Turn the mixture into a greased and lined 900g (2lb) loaf tin and bake in preheated oven 180C, 350F, Gas Mark 4 for at least an hour, testing with a skewer to see the cake is cooked right through the middle. Cool in tin. Freezes well.

HERBY CHEESE SCONES

These scones can be made in no time at all, and adding some herbs makes a change from the usual cheese scones, and I make a double batch and freeze them until required.

Makes about 12.

Ingredients:

50g (2oz) soft margarine
1 rounded teaspoon baking powder
75g (3oz) Cheddar cheese, grated
225g (8oz) self-raising flour
¼ teaspoon salt & ¼ teaspoon dry
    mustard sieved together

1 small egg
½ teaspoon mixed dried herbs
5 tablespoon milk
Milk to glaze

Put all the ingredients into a mixing bowl. Mix thoroughly to form a scone round. Turn onto a lightly floured surface. Roll out to 1cm (½ inch) thickness. Cut into rounds with a 5cm (2 inch) cutter. Brush the tops with milk and sprinkle a little grated cheese on top, put onto a baking sheet and bake in preheated oven 220C, 425F, Gas Mark 7 for 12-15 minutes.

GINGERNUTS

It's always handy to have some homemade biscuits in a tin to offer friends when they drop in unexpectedly for coffee.

Makes about 18 to 20 biscuits.

Ingredients:

225g (8oz) plain flour
110g (4oz) butter
1 small teaspoon bicarbonate of soda
225g (8oz) demerara Sugar

1 dessertspoon ground ginger
2 medium eggs, beaten
2 tablespoons milk

Dissolve soda in the milk and add the beaten eggs. Mix all the remaining ingredients together in a separate basin and rub in the butter until it resembles breadcrumbs. Add the milk, eggs and soda so that it blends together, and the mixture is soft and pliable. Then flour your hands and form the mixture into walnut sized balls and place them well apart on a greased baking sheet. Flatten tops a little. Bake in preheated oven 190C, 375F, Gas Mark 5 for 15 to 20 minutes.

GINGER CAKE

This is one of my favourite versions of gingercake. Best eaten with a proper tea on a freezing cold January day, to ward off those winter chills.

Serves 6.

Ingredients:

225g (8oz) self-raising flour
½ teaspoon bicarbonate of soda
½ teaspoon ground cinnamon
150ml (¼ pint) milk
2 tablespoons golden syrup

110g (4oz) soft brown sugar
2 teaspoon ground ginger
110g (4oz) butter
2 tablespoons black treacle
2 eggs

Preheat oven to 160/180C, 325-350F, Gas Mark 3-4, and grease a 20cm (8 inch) round cake tin. Mix all the dry ingredients together and sieve into a mixing bowl. In a pan, heat the butter, milk, treacle and syrup, stirring until all combined. Beat the eggs into the dry ingredients until well mixed and smooth. Then beat in treacle and syrup. Pour mixture into cake tin and bake for about 45 minutes until the top springs back when pressed. Cool in tin, turn out and then place in an airtight tin for a few days, to become moist. Or serve as a hot pudding with fromage frais or cream.

Contents – February

February

*T*he days start to get longer in February, and if the month lives up to its reputation it's usually wet and windy, and the kitchen is still one of the warmest places to be. It's the month for marmalade making, when those knarled skinned Seville oranges make their brief arrival from Spain towards the end of January to the beginning of February, and while the citrus season is coming to an end, lemons are still with us, although they may need an extra squeeze to provide enough juice for the Shrove Tuesday pancakes. February is a month when there isn't much home produced fruit, so it's a good time to cook some of the favourite traditional family puddings. Some days in February it seems as though spring is just around the corner, but then we get a few of those bitterly cold days, reminding us that we still need hot, warming, nourishing meals, and thick soups are still very much on the menu in my kitchen.

LENTIL SOUP

I've usually got a packet of lentils in my store cupboard, and I find this soup quick and easy to make. It heats up well and freezes too, but if you do freeze it, then remember to omit the curry powder until serving.

Serves 4-6.

Ingredients:

225g (8oz) red lentils
25g (1oz) butter
½ teaspoon mild curry powder (optional)

2 medium onions, peeled & sliced
1½ litres (2 pints) chicken cube stock

Wash lentils. Melt butter in heavy saucepan and let onion cook in it for about 5 minutes. Add lentils and stock and bring to the boil. Simmer for 1½ - 2 hours then add curry powder. Sieve or liquidise, reheat and serve sprinkled with chopped parsley.

BRUSSELS SPROUT SOUP

This soup has a delicious creamy smooth texture, and the Brussels Sprouts give it an unusual flavour. It's a good way of using up 'old' sprouts too!

Serves 4-6.

Ingredients:

450g (1lb) Brussels sprouts,
  cleaned & sliced
600ml (1 pint) chicken stock
  (cube will do)
1 medium onion, peeled & sliced

150ml (¼ pint) milk
25g (1oz) butter
1 tablespoon cream
¼ teaspoon nutmeg
Salt & pepper to taste

Heat butter in pan and fry onion until soft and golden, add Brussels sprouts and chicken stock. Cook until tender, about 25 minutes. Liquidise and return to pan, add milk and nutmeg. Season to taste, heat gently, and add cream when ready to serve.

MY FRENCH ONION SOUP

I first tasted French Onion Soup many years ago in France. My husband and I enjoyed it so much I devised my own recipe and have used it ever since – remember there weren't so many cookery books on the market then!

Serves 4.

Ingredients:

4 medium sized onions,
   peeled & chopped
600ml (1 pint) full cream milk
3 tablespoons grated Cheddar cheese
4 small, but fairly thick slices of hot toast

25g (1oz) butter
1 tablespoon flour
Breakfast cup hot water
Salt & pepper

Fry chopped onions in butter for 5 minutes. Stir in flour and seasoning and cook for a further 5 minutes. Gradually work in the hot water, stirring constantly until smooth. Simmer with lid on for about 10 minutes. Add milk and cook for a further 5 minutes. Put a slice of toast in each soup plate, pour the soup over, sprinkle cheese over and brown quickly under a hot grill.

STEAMED FISH PUDDING

Fish in a pudding is unusual, but it works, and makes a pleasant change in winter time from the more traditional steak and kidney pudding and meat pies. Try serving it with just one green vegetable, or puréed carrots and celeriac.

Serves 4-6.

Ingredients:

350g (12oz) fillets of white fish
450g (1lb) potatoes
75g (3oz) mild Cheddar cheese
Pepper & salt to taste

1 egg yolk
25g (1oz) butter
1 tablespoon chopped parsley
300ml (½ pint) shelled shrimps
   (or frozen, thawed)

Butter a plain mould thickly and line it with some of the fish fillets. Boil and mash the potatoes, adding the grated cheese, butter, and beaten egg yolk. Season to taste with chopped parsley, pepper and salt. Fill the lined mould alternately with layers of potato purée and shrimps. Fold remaining fillets of fish over the top. Cover with buttered paper and steam for ½ hour. Turn out and serve with shrimp or parsley sauce.

HERRING PASTIES WITH ORANGE MUSTARD SAUCE

These pasties make an ideal supper dish, and it's a change to have fish inside a pasty instead of meat. They take a little extra time and effort, but this is well worthwhile. You can eat them hot or cold, and if you don't want to use all the pasties, you can freeze what is left over.

Makes 8 pasties.

Ingredients:
8 herring fillets
175g (6oz) shortcrust pastry,
   frozen or homemade
Stuffing:
1 medium onion, peeled & chopped   25g (1oz) grated cheese
25g (1oz) white breadcrumbs   1 finely chopped clove of garlic
Pepper and salt   10g (½oz) butter
For the sauce:
10g (½oz) butter   1 dessertspoon plain flour
½ teaspoon mustard powder   Grated rind of the 2 oranges
Juice half a lemon   1 teaspoon sugar
1 dessertspoon chopped parsley   Pepper & salt
Juice of 2 large oranges
   (add water made up to 150ml) (¼ pint)

Mix all the stuffing ingredients together. Spread some on each fillet and roll them up. Roll out pastry on a floured surface and cut into 8 circles large enough to cover the herring rolls. Put the stuffed rolls on one half of the pastry, damp edges and fold over top half. Crimp edges together. Arrange on baking tray and bake in preheated oven 220C, 425F, Gas Mark 7 for 10 minutes, then reduce heat to 180C, 350F, Gas Mark 4 and bake for a further 15-20 minutes.
To make sauce while the pasties are cooking: Mix mustard and flour together. Melt butter and add flour, stir and cook for 3 minutes. Add orange and lemon juice gradually and bring to the boil. Simmer for 10-15 minutes. Add grated orange rind, parsley, sugar and seasoning to taste. Serve sauce separately with pasties.

BRAISED BEEF IN CIDER

I always cook casseroles in my Aga, and I prepare them early in the morning, pop them into the simmering oven, and leave them until needed for our evening meal. But if you are cooking by gas or electricity set your oven at the lowest temperature, which I've given below, and you will have the same results, a rich, thick gravy and tender juicy meat full of flavour. This casserole is particularly flavoursome – you can taste the cider in the gravy!

Serves 4.

Ingredients:

450g (1lb) topside of beef, cut into
   thin slices
1 tablespoon seasoned flour
700g (1½lb) onions, peeled & sliced
1 teaspoon dried thyme

1 bay leaf
35g (1½oz) beef dripping
300ml (½ pint) dry cider
Salt & pepper

Heat dripping in heavy frying pan. Coat slices of beef in seasoned flour and fry quickly for a few minutes until slices are browned on both sides, then place in casserole. Fry onions gently until soft and add to casserole with herbs and seasoning. Pour over cider and cover with lid. Cook in preheated oven 180C, 350F, Gas Mark 4 for 1½ - 2 hours until meat is tender. Or in a very slow oven 110C, 225F, Gas Mark ¼ for 5-6 hours, turning up to 130C, 250F, Gas Mark ½ for last hour of cooking. Add more cider if necessary during cooking time. Serve with mashed potatoes and green vegetable.

ROAST CHICKEN WITH SAGE BUTTER

You can use any herb of your choice, but I think sage goes well with chicken in winter time, and gives a lovely piquant flavour.

Serves 4-6.

Ingredients:

1 1.35kg (3lb) to 1.8kg (4lb) chicken,
   cleaned & with giblets removed
8-10 rashers of streaky bacon
1 heaped tablespoon chopped sage

175g (6oz) butter
Salt & pepper
300ml (½ pint) chicken stock
   (or chicken stock cube)

Soak giblets in salt water and set aside for gravy. Mix butter and sage together, and spread a little over the chicken, putting the remainder inside the bird. Sprinkle over seasoning and lay the bacon rashers over the chicken. Put chicken into a large meat tin, add stock and cook in preheated oven 190C, 375F, Gas Mark 5 for 1½ - 2 hours until bird is tender, basting occasionally. Wash giblets in salt water, drain and put them into a saucepan with enough water to cover. Simmer gently and then remove giblets, add liquid to pan with meat juices and thicken with a little cornflour. Serve with roast potatoes and broccoli.

SAVOURY STUFFED BREAST OF LAMB

If you get a really lean breast of lamb from your butcher, this can be one of the most nourishing dishes to cook in wintertime, and you can vary the stuffing you use according to your taste, and remember to ask your butcher to let you have the bones to use later for stock or soup.

Serves 4-6 (according to the size of your joint).

Ingredients:
1 boned breast of lamb
110g (4oz) pork sausage meat
1 dessertspoon chopped parsley
110g (4oz) dried apricots
  (or ready to use apricots)

1 small onion, peeled & chopped
50g (2oz) fresh white breadcrumbs
Seasoning

If using dried apricots then soak overnight, drain and cut into small pieces. Mix with onion, sausage meat, breadcrumbs and parsley and a little seasoning. Spread on meat, roll up and fasten with string or skewers. Roast in preheated oven 180C, 350F, Gas Mark 4, allowing 40 minutes per lb. Remove skewers before serving, and serve with broccoli in lemon butter, mint sauce or jelly, and a baked jacket potato.

BROCCOLI IN LEMON BUTTER

This also makes an excellent side vegetable dish to serve with fish or baked gammon.

Serves 6-8.

Ingredients:
1 kg (2¼lb) broccoli spears
50g (2oz) butter

Juice & finely grated rind of 1 lemon
Salt & freshly ground black pepper

Cook broccoli in boiling salted water until tender. Drain and set aside in a warm dish. Soften the butter and beat in lemon rind and juice. Season to taste and spoon over the hot broccoli.

BACON LOAF

If you're feeling a bit peckish and you have some of this loaf left over, then a slice cold or made into a sandwich is delicious.

Serves 4.

Ingredients:

350g (12oz) cooked bacon, minced
35g (1½oz) breadcrumbs, browned
½ teaspoon mixed herbs
50g (2oz) fresh white breadcrumbs
150ml (¼ pint) bacon stock

35g (1½oz) butter
1 large onion, finely chopped
½ teaspoon ground nutmeg
1 egg beaten
Pepper

Grease a 450g (1lb) loaf tin and press 25g (1oz) browned breadcrumbs round the bottom and sides. Heat butter in frying pan and fry onions until golden. Mix in the bacon and all remaining ingredients, adjusting seasoning and adding a little salt if necessary. Press the mixture into the loaf tin. Cover with foil and bake for 1 hour. Turn out and sprinkle with remaining breadcrumbs. Serve hot with sauté potatoes and green vegetables.

RUBY'S BREAD PUDDING

So named because it was one of Ruby's specialities. She would have a baking session most weekends, sausage rolls would be made, with rich flaky puff pastry that melted in your mouth, and a tray of Welsh cakes would be stacked and cooling on her kitchen table – Ruby was Welsh and excelled at making Welsh cakes – but it was her bread pudding that always caught my attention, and after sitting in her kitchen watching her make it on numerous occasions, I was able to memorize the ingredients and make it myself. Since then I've made it many times, especially in the winter months.

Serves 6-8.

Ingredients:

2 small loaves (one white
    and one brown, 2/3 days' old)
½ teaspoon salt (optional)
225g (8oz) butter
Sugar to taste

450g (1lb) mixed fruit
2 large eggs, beaten
½ teaspoon each of cinnamon, mixed
    spice & nutmeg

Cut crusts off the loaves of bread and soak bread in hot water. After 5 minutes put bread into a large sieve or colander and press out all the water. Then beat eggs into bread, add fruit and spices and put into a fairly large and deep meat tin. Cut butter into slices and lay on top of pudding and bake in a very slow oven, 140C, 275F, Gas Mark 1 for 3-4 hours until the pudding is golden brown and set. Serve hot with homemade custard, or on its own with a sprinkling of caster sugar. It keeps well and is delicious cut into slices cold.

FIG SPONGE PUDDING

A delicious light, fruity pudding – the added brandy gives it extra flavour and kick!

Serves 4-6.

Ingredients:

225g (8oz) dried figs	25g (1oz) raisins
25g (1oz) sultanas	75g (3oz) butter
75g (3oz) caster sugar	50g (2oz) self-raising flour
75g (3oz) fresh white breadcrumbs	25g (1oz) ground almonds
Pinch of cinnamon and nutmeg	Grated rind of ½ a lemon
1 egg	3 tablespoons brandy

Soak the figs and raisins overnight in cold, weak tea to which a little brandy has been added. Then drain the fruit and chop the figs finely. Cream butter and sugar together and fold in flour. Add breadcrumbs, ground almonds, spices, lemon rind and figs and dried fruit, stirring well. Beat the egg with brandy and add to the mixture. Turn into a 1½ litre (2 pint) buttered pudding basin and cover with buttered greaseproof paper and kitchen foil, or a pudding cloth. Cover and steam for 3-4 hours, keeping water topped up. When pudding is springy and risen, turn out on to a warm plate and serve with homemade custard or vanilla ice cream.

BANANA SURPRISE PUDDING

This pudding has a light and spongy texture, which is a change from the more heavier puddings we associate with winter, and children love it.

Serves 4.

Ingredients:

2 large or 3 small bananas	600ml (1 pint) milk
2 heaped tablespoons semolina	50g (2oz) caster sugar
A little lemon essence	A little apricot jam
1 lemon	1 tablespoon desiccated coconut

Make semolina mixture by taking a little of the milk and mixing cold with semolina and sugar. Bring remainder of the milk to the boil and pour on to the semolina mixture, adding a few drops of lemon essence. Return to the saucepan and cook slowly until it thickens, stirring well to avoid lumps. Line the bottom of an ovenproof dish with apricot jam. Over this spread a layer of prepared semolina. Slice bananas and thinly sprinkle with lemon juice and place on to semolina. Cover with another layer of semolina mixture. Sprinkle lightly with desiccated coconut and bake in a preheated oven 170C, 325F, Gas Mark 3 for 20-25 minutes until pale golden brown.

SHROVE TUESDAY PANCAKES

Shrove Tuesday nearly always falls in February, and it's still customary to remember this day by making and tossing pancakes, but these days, with recipes for all the different fillings around, I tend to make them throughout the year. However, I think the best pancakes are made using the basic ingredients and eaten with a squeeze of lemon juice, and a liberal sprinkling of caster sugar.

Makes about 12.

Ingredients:

10g (½oz) butter
300ml (½pint) milk
2 tablespoons caster sugar

110g (4oz) plain flour
2 eggs
Juice of 2 lemons

To make batter: Sieve the flour into a large mixing bowl and make a well in the centre. Beat eggs and milk, and sugar together until you have a smooth, creamy batter; leave to stand for at least an hour. Meanwhile heat a 18cm (7 inch) non-stick frying pan and pour enough pancake batter to coat the bottom. Allow 30 seconds for the pancake to brown on the underside, then turn over and cook until lightly coloured.

Carry on cooking the pancakes in this way, serving each one with a sprinkling of caster sugar and a squeeze of lemon juice. You can make the pancakes in advance, stack them interleaved with greaseproof paper, then reheat them in a warm oven.

DEVONSHIRE CREAM CAKE

I found this recipe in one of my old cookery notebooks, which must have been given to me by a friend or relative at some time or other. It's since been used by me countless times, in fact most weekends, when the ingredients can be doubled to make a large family cake. I've stuck to the original recipe here, but you can add 110g (4oz) dried fruit, or make a chocolate cake by substituting 25g (1oz) of flour with 25g (1oz) cocoa and icing the cake with melted dark chocolate.

Ingredients:

110g (4oz) butter, softened
110g (4oz) self-raising flour
½ teaspoon baking powder
Vanilla essence

110g (4oz) caster sugar
50g (2oz) cornflour
2 large eggs, beaten

Cream butter and sugar together. Then add beaten eggs. Add sifted flour, cornflour and vanilla essence. Gently fold in baking powder last. Spoon mixture into a greased and lined 450g (1lb) loaf tin and bake in a preheated oven 190C, 375F, Gas Mark 5 for about 30 minutes until very lightly golden on top. Cool and split cake in half and fill with butter cream and strawberry jam.

MARMALADE SLICES

These slices are ideal for packed lunches and picnics, and keep well stored in an airtight tin for at least a week, but they soon disappear from my kitchen unless I put them away quick!

Ingredients:

75g (3oz) butter or margarine
110g (4oz) porridge oats
25g (1oz) semolina or ground almonds

75g (3oz) soft brown sugar
1 tablespoon marmalade

Melt butter or margarine, sugar, marmalade, semolina or ground almonds in a saucepan. Take off the heat and stir in the porridge oats. Spoon into a greased Swiss roll or sandwich tin and bake in a preheated oven 190C, 375F, Gas Mark 5 for 25-30 minutes. Mark into slices while hot and leave in tin until cold.

CHOCOLATE CHESTNUT CAKE

I sometimes make this cake for special occasions, and it can be served as a pudding with a scoop of chocolate ice cream for each portion.

Serves 6.

Ingredients:

50g (2oz) butter
1 x 225g (8oz) tin chestnut purée
150ml (¼ pint) double cream
225g (8oz) plain chocolate
   wholemeal biscuits

25g (1oz) caster sugar
1 egg white
Grated chocolate to decorate

Crush the biscuits into crumbs. Melt butter with the sugar in a saucepan and mix in the biscuit crumbs. Press into a loose-bottomed 20.5cm (8 inch) cake tin and allow to cool. Whip egg white until stiff, whip cream lightly and stir into chestnut purée, and then fold in egg white; spoon chestnut mixture over biscuit base and chill. Decorate with grated chocolate.

FRUIT AND ALMOND SLICES

These almond slices have a surprise layer of fruit in the middle, which is a change from the more traditional layer of jam. They freeze well too.

Ingredients:

Bottom layer:
175g (6oz) plain flour
75g (3oz) hard margarine
50g (2oz) caster sugar
1 small egg & a little water to mix

Middle layer:
25g (1oz) glace cherries
25g (1oz) sultanas
110g (4oz) ground almond
110g (4oz) caster sugar
150g (5oz) soft margarine
2 eggs

Rub margarine into flour and add sugar. Add egg and a little water to mixture and stir well to make pastry. Roll out this mixture and line the base of a 30.5cm x 23cm (12 inch x 9 inch) baking tray. Prick base and bake in centre of preheated oven 180C, 350F, Gas Mark 4 for 10-15 minutes. While base is cooking whisk topping ingredients together until light and fluffy. When base is cooked remove from oven and sprinkle with cherries and sultanas, then gently spread sponge mixture over the fruit. Return to the oven and bake at same temperature for 30-40 minutes. Cool in tin, and cut into slices.

SEVILLE MARMALADE

The Seville orange season is a short one, so keep a sharp look-out for them in the shops when they start to arrive at the end of January and carry on into the month of February. If you don't want to make a large quantity of marmalade in one go, then it's useful to freeze some oranges and make another batch later on.

Yields 2¼ kg (5lb)

Ingredients:
700g (1½lb) Seville oranges
Juice of 1 large lemon

1½ litres (2 pints) water
1.35kg (3lb) granulated sugar

Wash and put the fruit whole and unpeeled into a large saucepan or preserving pan. Pour on 1½ litres (2 pints) boiling water and simmer gently with the lid on until the fruit is tender. When the fruit is cooked and tender cut it in half, remove pips, and finely cut up the fruit, carefully retaining all the juice. Return pips to the water in which the fruit was cooked and boil for 5 minutes to extract more pectin. Strain pips from liquid and return the sliced fruit and lemon juice to the preserving pan. Reduce heat, add the sugar and stir until dissolved. Bring to the boil and boil rapidly until setting point is reached, testing a little on a saucer. Pot into warm jars and seal.

31

Contents – March

March

March is a month of change and while it brings longer days and bright spells, bitter winds and driving rain can still remind us that winter hasn't yet given way to spring, even though warmer weather is just around the corner. So it's still a time for hot food and hearty cooking, and making soups that are quick and easy to prepare. Trees are now starting to show their buds, and the ground is beginning to dry out ready for spring planting. Spring cabbages are full of flavour during March – try shredding and gently steaming them, served lightly buttered and topped with toasted cashew nuts they make a delicious second vegetable. Fruit stalls continue to provide a colourful display of citrus fruit, and fresh pineapples are good value this month (see the delicious pineapple recipe in this chapter). It's the start of the salmon season, and white fish should be arriving plump and plentiful.

PEA SOUP

When I'm in a hurry and want to make a soup quick, I find this recipe invaluable. I usually have most of the ingredients to hand, and can assemble it in next to no time.

Serves 4-6.

Ingredients:

1 medium sized packet of frozen peas
1 medium onion, peeled & chopped
600ml (1 pint) chicken stock
  (or water & stock cube)
50g (2oz) butter
300ml (½ pint) creamy milk
Double cream to garnish (optional)
  or use chopped parsley

Melt butter in a pan and sweat onion for a few minutes. Add peas, stock and milk and cook gently until peas are tender. Liquidise and season to taste. Serve piping hot with a blob of cream on each helping, or garnish with chopped parsley.

CARROT SOUP

This soup is a good way of using up 'old carrots', and the swirl of cream on top gives it a professional look. It freezes well, but don't add the cream until it's needed.

Serves 4-6.

Ingredients:

450g (1lb) old carrots
50g (2oz) butter
A little cream
Parsley for garnishing
3 small onions
150ml (¼ pint) milk
Salt & pepper to taste
425ml (¾ pint) chicken stock
  (made with stock cube)

Peel the carrots and scrape them coarsely. Peel and slice onions. Melt the butter in a pan and fry the carrots and onions over a low heat for 5-10 minutes. Add stock, salt and pepper and cook for 15 minutes. If you want a smooth soup, then blend the soup in a blender, or alternatively, you can cook for another 10 minutes. Take off heat and stir in milk, but do not boil. Serve with a swirl of cream and sprinkle with chopped parsley.

SMOKED SALMON MOUSSE

This must be one of quickest starters on record, and it also makes a tasty meal for lunch served with a green salad and brown bread and butter.

Serves 4.

Ingredients:

225g (8oz) smoked salmon
110g (4oz) Philadelphia cream cheese
A little paprika
110g (4oz) carton soured cream
Juice of ½ lemon

Just mix all the above ingredients together in a liquidizer until they are smooth and creamy. Serve with toast or brown bread and butter.

LIVER PATÉ

This paté is delicious served with rolls of fried bacon on toast or as a filling for rolls, and it can be stored in the refrigerator for up to 1-2 weeks, or in the deep freeze for 1-2 months.

Serves 4.

Ingredients:

225g (8oz) pig's liver
1 medium onion
A little garlic powder (optional)
225g (8oz) belly pork
1 teaspoon each salt & pepper

Mince liver with onion, and mince pork separately. Then mix together thoroughly with seasoning. Press mixture into a fireproof dish and bake in a very slow oven, 150C, 300F, Gas Mark 2 for about 1 hour, taking care not to brown top too much. You can bake paté in small foil dishes if you are going to store or freeze it.

QUICK ITALIAN SPAGHETTI

Adding chilli powder and cinnamon to the spaghetti gives it a real spicy flavour, with the olives adding a real Mediterranean touch to the dish.

Serves 4-6.

Ingredients:

3 medium onions, peeled & chopped
1 x 425g (15oz) can of tomatoes
½ teaspoon cinnamon
1 x 425g (15oz) can of tomato
  soup (condensed)
Boiled spaghetti, allow 75g
  (3oz) to 110g (4oz) per person

2 tablespoons vegetable oil
450g (1lb) minced beef
½ teaspoon chilli powder
Salt & pepper to taste
Chopped stuffed olives

Heat oil in a large pan and fry onion and meat until browned. Then add soup, tomatoes, chilli powder, cinnamon and salt and pepper. Simmer covered for 1½ hours. Just before serving add the chopped olives, and spoon the sauce over each portion of the spaghetti.

BACON JOINT IN SOMERSET CIDER

This recipe calls for collar or shoulder, but I always think collar has a sweeter taste when cooked. This joint can be eaten hot or cold, and if you are going to eat it cold, you will find that by leaving it in the baking tin and spooning the juices over – will keep it moist and succulent.

Serves 6.

Ingredients:

1.8kg (4lb) bacon joint (collar
  or shoulder)
300ml (½ pint) rough draught cider
50g (2ozs) Demerara sugar mixed with
  25g (1oz) fine brown breadcrumbs

6 cloves
1 large orange

Soak the collar in cold water overnight. Drain and place the bacon in a large meat tin. Sprinkle the juice and grated rind of the orange over the joint and add cloves and cider. Bake in preheated oven 180C, 350F, Gas Mark 4 for about 1 hour, basting frequently with cider and juices. Remove the skin and if it comes off easily you will know the bacon is cooked. Sprinkle the joint with sugar and crumbs and bake for the remainder of time. You should end up with a nice moist and tasty joint.

LIVER AND BACON HOT POT

March can be a cold month and this is a nourishing dish to banish those winter chills away.

Serves 4-6.

Ingredients:

450g (1lb) ox liver	50g-75g (2oz-3oz) bacon slices
225g (½lb) onions, peeled & sliced	A little beef dripping
1.35kg (3lb) potatoes, peeled & sliced	Salt & pepper

Wash and slice liver. Put into a deep pie dish with alternate layers of sliced bacon, onions and potatoes, seasoning each layer. Finish with a layer of potatoes and half fill the dish with vegetable stock cube and water. Bake in preheated oven 190C, 375F, Gas Mark 5 for 1½-2 hours until potatoes are nicely browned on top. Serve with cooked butter beans and creamed carrots.

CHICKEN AND HERB PUDDING

This pudding is well worth the effort of the extra time it takes to put together, and if you don't want the bother of boning the chicken, then you can use chicken joints instead.

Serves 4.

Ingredients:

1kg (2¼lb) chicken, skinned & boned (or chicken joints)	350g (12oz) self-raising flour
	Stick of celery
225g (8oz) belly pork	2 tablespoons chopped parsley
225g (8oz) small shallots or onions	2 teaspoons mixed dried herbs
175g (6oz) shredded suet	Salt & pepper

Cube the pork. Put the carcass of the chicken with the skin in a large saucepan, cover with water and add a stick of celery and one onion, salt and pepper, cover and simmer for 1½-2 hours. Make the suet pastry in the usual way and line a 1½ litre (2 pint) basin, reserving enough for the top. Cut the chicken into small pieces. Sauté the cubed pork and onion. Put a layer of chicken into the bottom of the pastry lined basin, then a layer of pork and onion. Pour in a little of the reduced chicken stock. Season well. Sprinkle over half the parsley and a little marjoram. Finish with a layer of chicken. Arrange the remaining onions and herbs around the top. Cover with pastry lid. Seal well. Put a buttered paper on top, then foil. Cook in a pan of water or a steamer for 3 hours. Thicken the remaining chicken stock and use as gravy when serving pudding. Serve with vegetables of your choice.

LEEK AND BACON QUICHE

Most flans and quiches call for eggs and cream, but this one is different in that it doesn't, and when it's baked you end up with pastry that is crisp and golden brown. It can be eaten either hot or cold, and you can also make small tartlets for a tasty snack.

Serves 8.

Ingredients:

3-4 rashers of back bacon
3 leeks, cleaned & thinly sliced across
150ml (¼ pint) milk
Grated Gruyere cheese

50g (2oz) butter
1 tablespoon flour
Black pepper

Line a 23cm (9 inch) - 25.5cm (10 inch) flan dish with shortcrust pastry. Melt butter in saucepan. Add diced bacon and cook until crisp, then add leeks to pan and stir well. Season with a little ground black pepper, cover and cook slowly for 10 minutes. Stir in flour and add milk, stirring until sauce boils and thickens. Pour into flan case, sprinkle with grated cheese and bake in a hot preheated oven 200C, 400F, Gas Mark 6 for about ½ hour. Serve with a green salad.

PINEAPPLE MERINGUE

This pudding makes a change from the more traditional lemon meringue pie, and it's very low in calories too, if you're counting!

Serves 4.

Ingredients:

1 pineapple
1 small tin grapefruit segments
2 egg whites

1 eating apple
Almond flakes
4 tablespoons caster sugar

Scoop out half the pineapple and mix with the other fruits. Whisk egg whites and fold in sugar. Fill the halved pineapple with fruit and pile the meringue on top. Sprinkle on the almond flakes and bake for 15 minutes at 180C, 350F, Gas Mark 4.

FRUITY RICE PUDDING

This is a different and interesting version of the ordinary rice pudding most of us remember from our childhood days. It can cook in a very slow oven while you are cooking a casserole for a main dish.

Serves 4.

Ingredients:
50g (2oz) rice	50g (2oz) granulated sugar
25g (1oz) butter	600ml (1 pint) milk
25g (1oz) seedless raisins & sultanas	Rind of 1 orange
25g (1oz) chopped glace cherries & angelica	25g (1oz) candied peel

Put milk, rice, sugar and butter into a deep greased pie dish. Stir in the fruit and finely grated orange rind. Cook very slowly in a preheated oven 150C, 300F, Gas Mark 2 for about 2 hours. Stir a couple of times during cooking. This pudding can look attractive with a meringue topping, made with 2 egg whites and 110g (4oz) caster sugar, piled on top of pudding and cooked during the last ½ hour of cooking time.

BANANA AND LEMON CREAM JELLY

It makes a pleasant change to have a light creamy dessert to go with the more heavier main meals we eat in the colder months of the year, but don't keep it too long as the banana tends to discolour.

Serves 6.

Ingredients:
1 lemon jelly	4 medium bananas
150ml (¼ pint) double cream	A little vegetable oil
A round cake tin 20.5cm (8 inch) diameter	

Make up the jelly as directed on the packet, using 425ml (¾ pint) boiling water. Leave until jelly is almost cold. Rub a few drops of cooking oil round the inside of the cake tin. Pour a little of the cooled jelly into the tin to just cover the base, then put it into the refrigerator to set. Peel and slice one banana and arrange 6 slices on top of the jelly in the base of the tin. Run over just enough jelly to cover them and leave again to set, leaving about one third of a pint of the jelly. Peel remaining bananas and mash with a fork. Whip double cream and then fold into mashed bananas, adding the rest of jelly. Pour this gently on to the jelly and bananas in the tin and leave to set. When ready to serve loosen jelly around the top with a knife then quickly dip the base of the tin into hot water to ease jelly. Carefully turn out on to a serving plate and decorate with a little cream.

CHOCOLATE SPICE LOAF

This is an unusual cake, and the recipe was given to me by a friend who visited Holland and brought it back with her. When cooked it's a nice moist cake and keeps well. You can serve it either plain or buttered.

Ingredients:

3 medium eggs, beaten
175g (6oz) self-raising flour
4 tablespoons lemon juice
1 level tablespoon ground mixed spice

175g (6oz) soft brown sugar
6 tablespoons milk
110g (4oz) chocolate, grated
175g (6oz) butter softened, or
   soft margarine

To complete top of cake:

1 tablespoon apricot jam &
   chocolate vermicelli

Beat eggs with sugar in large mixing bowl until pale. Melt butter gently in a pan and add to the egg and sugar mixture. Sift the flour, mixed spice and a pinch of salt into the mixing bowl, and stir into the mixture. Heat the milk until lukewarm and add to the mixture with the lemon juice and chocolate. Mix thoroughly together and pour into a greased and lined 23cm x 10cm x 7.5cm (9 inch by 4 inch by 3 inch) loaf tin. Bake in the centre of preheated oven 180C, 350F, Gas Mark 4 for 1-1½ hours – test with a skewer to make sure it is cooked right through the centre. Cool for 5 minutes in tin then turn out on cooling rack. Melt the apricot jam and brush it over the top of the warm loaf. Decorate the edges with the chocolate vermicelli. This cake freezes very well.

GARIBALDI SLICES

So called because they contain currants and resemble the commercially sold biscuits. It's a very quick all-in-one recipe and very much resembles a shortbread mixture, and you can add chopped apricots or any other dried fruit you enjoy as an alternative to currants.

Makes 12-15 slices.

Ingredients:

110g (4oz) plain flour
110g (4oz) soft brown sugar
110g (4oz) softened butter, or
   soft margarine

110g (4oz) fine semolina
110g (4oz) currants

Put all the ingredients into a large mixing bowl and beat vigorously either with a wooden spoon or a food mixer until mixture resembles large breadcrumbs. Grease and line a large Swiss roll tin and press mixture into tin. Bake in preheated oven 190C, 375F, Gas Mark 5 for 15-20 minutes, or until golden brown. Sprinkle with caster sugar while still hot and mark into slices. Remove from tin when completely cold.

MALT LOAF

When I'm having a baking session I sometimes have an urge to make homemade bread and fruit loaves. This malt loaf is one of my favourites, it doesn't take long to make and always comes out of the oven baked to perfection, and is a great teatime family favourite.

Ingredients:

225g (8oz) sultanas
50g (2oz) mixed dried peel
300ml (½ pint) water
½ teaspoon bicarbonate of soda
225g (8oz) soft, dark brown sugar
2 tablespoons malt extract

225g (8oz) raisins
75g (3oz) butter
350g (12oz) self-raising flour
Pinch of salt
2 large eggs, beaten

Put all the dried fruit into a large saucepan with the butter and water, and bring to the boil. Simmer for 5-10 minutes and allow to cool. Sift the flour, bicarbonate of soda and salt together into a large mixing bowl and stir in the sugar. Pour in the warm fruit mixture and add the beaten eggs and malt extract. Mix thoroughly. Pour into 2 greased and lined 450g (1lb) loaf tins and bake in preheated oven 180C, 350F, Gas Mark 4 for 30 minutes, then move to a lower shelf and bake for a further 30 minutes, or until a skewer comes out clean when tested. Allow to cool for about 5 minutes. Delicious eaten warm and spread with butter.

Contents – April

April

*E*aster usually arrives sometime during April, bringing its unpredictable mixture of showers and sunshine, which heralds the arrival of spring. Hot cross buns, and freshly baked biscuits and cakes make it an ideal time for gathering friends around the table to sample your Easter baking, and this month we catch our first whiff of spring, and our meals become lighter. New arrivals on the market include an increased variety of salads and imported tomatoes. In this chapter I am including traditional spring lamb recipes, which I like to cook, and chicken, which is in season all the year round, and today there is ample choice, from the ordinary free range, to the organic free range and the yellow corn fed. I've also included some mouth-watering recipes for Easter tea, and some perfect puddings to serve with your Easter lunch.

POTATO AND CELERY SOUP

Even with the milder weather it's still nice to have a warm soup, which you can always follow with a light, or cold, lunch.

Serves 6.

Ingredients:

2 medium onions, peeled & chopped	600ml (1 pint) water
300ml (½ pint) milk	10g (½oz) butter
1 bay leaf	10g (½oz) plain flour
1 tablespoon chopped parsley	Salt & pepper to taste
450g (1lb) old potatoes, peeled & sliced	3 stalks of celery, cleaned & finely chopped

Melt the butter in pan and fry the chopped vegetables lightly for a few minutes. Put the vegetables into a large saucepan and add the water and bay leaf. Bring to the boil and simmer for about 30 minutes until the potatoes are thoroughly cooked. Mix the flour with the milk and add to the soup, stirring constantly. Season to taste, and sprinkle with parsley when ready to serve.

HUNTER'S PATÉ

This paté is a good standby to have in the freezer, it makes a delicious starter and serves as a quick lunch spread on fingers of toast or oatcakes.

Serves 4-6.

Ingredients:

450g (1lb) chopped chicken livers	175g (6oz) cooked ham
1 onion, finely chopped	1 clove garlic, finely chopped
75g (3oz) butter	2 tablespoons olive oil
3 tablespoons whisky or sherry	3 tablespoons single cream
Salt & pepper	

Lightly fry onion and garlic until soft. Add chicken livers and seasoning, and fry until cooked. Put into a food processor with the cooked ham, cream and whisky. Blend for a few seconds. Place in a bowl and refrigerate for 2-3 days before serving. Serves 4 with fingers of toast or oatcakes. This paté freezes well.

CHICKEN SALAD

This makes an excellent first course for 8, or a main course for 4, and served in a glass salad bowl it looks attractive and colourful.

Ingredients:

450g (1lb) cooked chicken, chopped
25g (1oz) chopped blanched almonds
Juice of ½ lemon
4 tablespoons mayonnaise

1 grapefruit,
½ cucumber
Black pepper
1 tablespoon chopped parsley

Put chopped chicken into a glass salad bowl and cover with lemon juice and black pepper. Remove rind and pith from grapefruit, and cut into small pieces. Peel and chop cucumber. Mix in the almonds and mayonnaise. Decorate with chopped parsley and chill well.

ROAST LEG OF LAMB WITH ROSEMARY & GARLIC

Herbs and sweet tender lamb with vegetables can all be cooked together in this recipe. Choose a fairly large attractive casserole dish so that you can serve it straight from oven to table.

Serves 6.

Ingredients:

1.6kg (3½lb) leg of lamb
2 cloves of garlic cut into slivers
14 shallots
350g (12oz) small carrots, peeled
1 tablespoon cornflour
350g (12oz) mushrooms, cleaned & sliced
200ml (7fl oz) chicken stock
  (stock cube will do)
1.35kg (3lb) small potatoes,
  peeled & halved

Sprig of rosemary
2 tablespoons olive oil
75ml (3fl oz) red wine
1 teaspoon red wine vinegar
2 tablespoons cold water
Freshly ground black pepper
450g (1lb) courgettes, trimmed &
  cut into chunks

Make several slits in the lamb and insert slivers of garlic and rosemary. Heat oil in large flameproof casserole and brown lamb all over. Add shallots and cook until golden brown. Pour over red wine and chicken stock, cover casserole with a well fitting lid and simmer on a low heat for 2 hours, adding more stock if necessary. Add carrots and potatoes to casserole and stir in wine vinegar. Cover and simmer for a further 25 minutes. Blend cornflour with water and stir into juices until thickened. Add courgettes and mushrooms, cover and simmer for another 15 minutes. Season to taste. Carve lamb into thick slices and serve with the cooked vegetables.

LAMB IN LEMON SAUCE

One of my favourite recipes, the taste of lemon and herbs coming through the creamy sauce, makes an excellent combination.

Serves 4-6.

Ingredients:

700g (1½lb) boned shoulder or leg of lamb, cut into 2.5cm (1 inch) cubes
50g (2oz) unsmoked gammon, chopped
1 medium onion, peeled & chopped

25g (1oz) lard or cooking oil
2 tablespoon flour
Salt & pepper

For the sauce:

4 tablespoons dry white wine
300ml (½ pint) stock (lamb cube will do)
2 tablespoons lemon juice
1 tablespoon chopped parsley

2 egg yolks
1 teaspoon marjoram
½ teaspoon grated lemon rind

Melt lard or oil in heavy pan, add gammon, lamb and onion and fry gently for 10 minutes. Sprinkle in the flour and season to taste with salt and pepper. Cook, stirring for 1 minute. Add wine and bring back to the boil, and boil until reduced by half. Add the stock and bring back to the boil, stirring. Cover and simmer for 45 minutes, or until the lamb is tender. Skim off any surface fat. In a bowl beat together the egg yolks, lemon juice, rind and herbs. Add 3 tablespoons of cooking liquor and blend well. Add to the pan and stir until the sauce thickens (do not boil). Serve with noodles or new potatoes.

ROAST CHICKEN WITH GARLIC & ROSEMARY

In this recipe I've combined plenty of garlic and rosemary, which produces a wonderful flavour.

Serves 6.

Ingredients:

1 chicken 2.25kg-2.7kg (5lb-6lb)
4 teaspoons fresh chopped rosemary
2 tablespoons oil

4 garlic bulbs
1 lemon
50g (2oz) butter

Separate garlic cloves, leave unpeeled, and put all but 8 into a roasting tin with oil, and roast for 25 minutes, until soft. Then peel cloves, season and mash to a purée, add grated zest of lemon and a little juice, combine with rosemary. Loosen skin on chicken breasts and spread this mixture between the skin and flesh. Drizzle over the melted butter, and add more seasoning. Put the remaining 8 cloves on the outside of the chicken between the leg and breast, and put the remaining lemon zest inside the cavity. Roast chicken in preheated oven 190C, 375F, Gas Mark 5, positioning on right breast for 30 minutes, turning onto left breast for a further 30 minutes, then turn chicken on its back and roast for another 35-45 minutes until it's cooked and the outside is crispy and golden.

ROAST SPRING VEGETABLES

When it comes to vegetables, nothing can beat fresh greens, and all sorts of baby vegetables are available at this time of the year. In this recipe you can choose from onions, peppers, courgettes, carrots or broccoli florets and spring onions.

Serves 6-8.

Ingredients:
900g (2lb) mixed baby vegetables   2½ tablespoons olive oil
Fresh ground black pepper

Cut broccoli into small florets, peel baby onions and clean and trim other vegetables. Pour oil into a large roasting tin 25 minutes before you are ready to serve chicken, and heat for 5 minutes. Add vegetables and cook for 20-25 minutes turning and basting occasionally. Goes well with the garlic and rosemary chicken.

RASPBERRY PAVLOVA

This is the perfect pudding for your Easter lunch, and it's quick and easy to prepare.

Serves 6-8.

Ingredients:
4 egg whites   225g (8oz) caster sugar
½ teaspoon vanilla essence   1 teaspoon vinegar
1 teaspoon cornflour   25g (1oz) flaked almonds
225g (8oz) frozen raspberries (thawed)   300ml (½ pint) whipped cream

Draw a 20.5cm (8 inch) circle on non-stick paper and place on baking tray. Whisk egg whites until stiff and standing in peaks. Beat in sugar, 1 tablespoon at a time. Fold in vanilla essence, vinegar and cornflour. Spoon meringue mixture over the round on the non-stick paper, making a slight hollow in centre. Bake in preheated oven 130C, 250F, Gas Mark ½ for 1 hour or until firm. Leave to cool. Then carefully remove non-stick paper, place on a serving plate and fill the hollow with the whipped cream and thawed raspberries, sprinkle with flaked almonds.

BREAD AND BUTTER PUDDING

Adding cherries and angelica to this pudding was the only way I could get my daughter, when she was small, to eat it. The red and green colours made it attractive and the sprinkling of sugar mixed with coconut made it nice and crunchy.

Ingredients:

3 thin slices bread & butter
50g (2oz) sugar
50g (2oz) sultanas
25g (1oz) angelica, chopped

600ml (1 pint) milk
2 large eggs, beaten
25g (1oz) glacé cherries, quartered
1 tablespoon sugar & 1 tablespoon
    coconut for sprinkling

Mix the eggs with milk and sugar. Pour into a 850ml (1½ pint) ovenproof dish. Cut bread into small squares. Put fruit into the milk mixture, reserving some for topping. Add bread squares on top and cook in preheated oven 170C, 325F, Gas Mark 3 for 1½ hours, until set. Sprinkle reserved fruit on top and sprinkle with mixed sugar and coconut. Cook for a further 10 minutes until topping is golden brown and crunchy.

BAKEWELL TART

I usually cheat when making this tart and use ready-made shortcrust pastry, but for those of you who wish to make your own pastry I have given the ingredients you will need.

Serves 4-6.

Ingredients:

225g (8oz) plain flour
¼ teaspoon salt
110g (4oz) butter
4 tablespoons cold water

For filling:

50g (2oz) caster sugar
A little almond flavouring
1 egg
50g (2oz) butter
Strawberry or raspberry jam
50g (2oz) breadcrumbs
A little lemon juice
Ground almonds

Sift flour and salt into a mixing bowl. Add butter and cut up into small pieces with a knife. Rub in with fingertips until it resembles fine breadcrumbs. Add water and mix to a stiff paste using a knife. Turn out onto a floured board, shape and roll out to required thickness. Line a pie plate with the pastry. Cover with a layer of jam, and then a layer of ground almonds. Cream butter and sugar together and beat in egg and breadcrumbs, add almond essence and lemon juice. Spread the mixture over the pastry. Bake in preheated oven 190C, 375F, Gas Mark 5 for 25-30 minutes.

RHUBARB CAKE

Forced rhubarb may still be around, but I think the greener outdoor fruit gives a real sharp rhubarb taste. This easy to bake sweet tangy sponge cake has a crumbly almond and sugar topping. It keeps well in a tin for 3-4 days, and also makes a delicious pudding served warm with cream or a thick yoghurt.

Serves 6-8.

Ingredients:
560g (1¼ lb) rhubarb
150g (5oz) caster sugar
Pinch of salt
200g (7oz) plain flour
75g (3oz) cornflour
Icing sugar for dusting

200g (7oz) butter
Few drops of vanilla essence
2 medium eggs
1 teaspoon baking powder
75g (3oz) ground almonds

Preheat oven to 180C, 350F, Gas Mark 4. Cut rhubarb into 2.5cm (1 inch) chunks. Cream 110g (4oz) butter with two thirds of the sugar, vanilla essence and salt until fluffy. Gently stir in beaten eggs. Mix the flour with the baking powder and half the cornflour and fold into creamed mixture. Add half the ground almonds. Grease a 23cm (9 inch) spring-form cake tin. Put cake mixture in tin, smooth over and arrange the rhubarb on top. Rub together remaining sugar, butter, almonds and cornflour. Spread crumble mixture over the rhubarb. Bake on the lowest shelf for about 75 minutes until firm and golden. Cool and dust with icing sugar before serving.

SPICY EASTER TEABREAD

This tea bread improves with keeping, but it doesn't last long in my family! I've used sultanas and dates in this recipe, but you can use any fruit you may have in your store cupboard, and adding half a grated apple keeps it moist and fresh.

Ingredients:
225g (8oz) self-raising flour
½ teaspoon ground cinnamon
75g (3oz) caster sugar
50g (2oz) dates, chopped
6 tablespoons milk

1 teaspoon mixed spice
75g (3oz) butter, softened
50g (2oz) sultanas
1 egg, beaten

Preheat oven 190C, 375F, Gas Mark 5. Grease and line a 900g (2lb) loaf tin. Mix together flour and spices. Chop butter into small pieces and cut roughly into flour with a knife. Add sugar, sultanas, dates, egg and milk, and mix to a soft consistency. Turn into prepared tin and bake for 40-45 minutes until a skewer comes out clean. Remove from oven and turn out on to a wire rack to cool. Delicious sliced and buttered.

PINEAPPLE CAKE

Simnel cakes were traditionally baked and given on Mothering Sunday so that they could be kept for the remainder of Lent and eaten at Easter, but I prefer a less rich cake. This recipe uses pineapple and marzipan, and the top is iced, but if you prefer, you can always cover the top with marzipan instead of icing, making it more traditional.

Ingredients:

175g (6oz) butter	175g (6oz) caster sugar
110g (4oz) marzipan	3 eggs
3 rings canned pineapple	75g (3oz) plain flour
75g (3oz) cornflour	½ teaspoon baking powder
Apricot jam	Glacé cherries
White fondant icing (or thick glace)	

Cream butter and sugar until soft, add marzipan and continue beating until mixture is well blended. Add eggs, beating well. Drain pineapple and chop 2 rings into small pieces. Add this to the creamed mixture. Sift flour, cornflour and baking powder together and fold into mixture. Turn into a small loaf tin or a 15cm-18cm (6-7inch) cake tin and bake in preheated oven 190C, 375F, Gas Mark 5 for 1-1½ hours. Turn out and cool on wire rack. When cold spread with sieved apricot jam, cover with icing and decorate with remaining pineapple ring cut into two and glacé cherries.

HOT CROSS BUNS

Easter wouldn't be Easter without Hot Cross Buns! And these days I find the easy blend yeasts convenient and quick to use. Hot cross buns are always best eaten on the day they are made, but if you have any left over they are delicious toasted.

Makes 12.

Ingredients:

450g (1lb) plain flour
1 sachet easy blend yeast
1 teaspoon cinnamon
50g (2oz) caster sugar
25g (1oz) sultanas
1 egg, beaten
50g (2oz) strong plain flour

75g (3oz) butter, diced
1 teaspoon salt
1½ teaspoon mixed spice
50g (2oz) currants
25g (1oz) mixed chopped peel
300ml (½ pint) warm milk

For the glaze:

4 tablespoons each milk & water mixed   3 tablespoons caster sugar

Sift flour into a warm mixing bowl. Rub in butter, and then stir in the yeast, salt, spices, sugar, fruit and peel, mixing well. Add the egg and enough milk to mix to a smooth dough. Turn onto a floured surface and knead for 5 minutes. Divide dough into 12 and roll into rounds. Place well spaced on an oiled baking sheet. Leave, covered with a tea towel, in a warm place for about 1 hour to double in size. Make a dough with plain flour and a little water. Roll out thinly and cut into strips. Using a little water affix pastry crosses onto the risen buns. Bake in preheated oven 200C, 400F, Gas Mark 6 for 15-20 minutes until golden brown, cool on wire rack. Heat milk and water with sugar until sugar dissolves, then brush over the warm buns. Leave to dry for a few minutes, then glaze again. Serve warm.

EASTER BISCUITS

I bake biscuits all year round, but these Easter Biscuits are just that little bit special, with extra spices and fruit, and added brandy, they become almost luxurious!

Makes about 15.

Ingredients:

75g (3oz) caster sugar
1 egg yolk
175g (6oz) plain flour
½ level teaspoon each cinnamon
   & ginger
50g (2oz) currants
25g (1oz) chopped mixed peel

75g (3oz) unsalted butter
2 tablespoons brandy
½ level teaspoon baking powder
1 pinch salt
50g (2oz) sultanas
1 egg white
Caster sugar for dredging

Beat together butter and sugar until light and fluffy. Beat in 1 egg yolk, and then beat in brandy. Sift together flour, baking powder, salt, cinnamon and ginger. Fold this mixture into wet mixture. Add currants, sultanas and peel. Place in a plastic bag and refrigerate for 1 hour. Remove dough and give a gentle knead. Roll out on a well-floured surface to 3mm (⅛th) thickness. Cut into rounds with a 6cm (2½ inch) cutter. Place rounds on a greased baking tray. Place in centre of preheated oven 200C, 400F, Gas Mark 6 and bake for 10 minutes. Brush top of biscuits with egg white and dredge surface lightly with caster sugar, and bake for a further 9-10 minutes until golden brown. Cool and place in an airtight tin when cold.

SUFFOLK RUSKS

When I'm having a baking session I like to make some rusks, and I try to keep a supply in my cake tin for unexpected guests. You can serve them warmed up for tea with butter and jam, or they can be eaten cold with cheese and butter.

Ingredients:
450g (1lb) plain flour
2 egg yolks
Large pinch of salt

75g (3oz) butter
4 teaspoons baking powder
Milk & water (half & half)

Rub butter into the flour. Add baking powder and salt, and stir well. Add beaten egg yolks and enough milk and water to bind. Roll out. Cut into rounds the size of a sherry glass top and place close together on a well-greased baking sheet. Bake in preheated oven 180C, 350F, Gas Mark 4 until pale brown. Remove and cut in half. Replace in oven until well browned and crisp.

BREAD ROLLS

You can serve these rolls hot, instead of potatoes, with salads and cold meats. Make a double batch and you can freeze them to take on picnics when the warmer weather arrives.

Ingredients:
900g (2lb) strong plain flour
600ml (1 pint) water
A little sugar

1 packet dried yeast
25g (1oz) margarine

Put 4 tablespoons of the warm water in a small bowl with a tablespoon of sugar. Sprinkle on the dried yeast, stirring. Put aside to activate. Rub margarine into the flour. Add yeast and the rest of the water. Knead well. Set aside to rise in a warm place for about 1 hour. Shape into small round knobs. Put on a greased baking tin, leave 10 minutes and bake in preheated oven 200C, 400F, Gas Mark 6 for about 15-20 minutes.

Contents – May

May

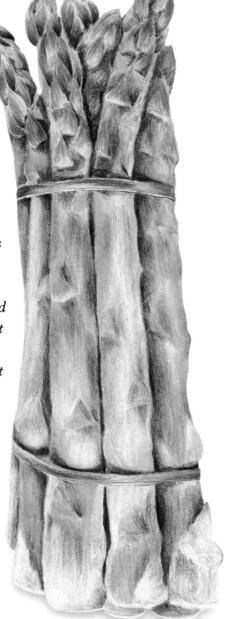

May is a month full of promise, with the excitement of summer just around the corner, but the month is still very much a part of spring. Crops begin to benefit from the warmer weather, and it's a time to enjoy the bounty of all the fresh young vegetables, which are now beginning to make their appearance on market stalls and in shops. New carrots are delicious eaten raw with their feathery tops attached, and it's the start of our own asparagus season – short and sweet – so I always try to make the most of it by making it into flans and soups, and gently steamed with a little butter it can make a light lunch served with brown bread and butter. And, if you're lucky, you may hear the cuckoo calling, although as I write I haven't heard him yet this month, but my husband tells me that he has heard him several times – so maybe the cuckoo is telling us that summer is about to begin!

MELON WITH PARMA HAM

Melons are refreshing and juicy and quite cheap to buy during the summer months, and this starter can be made in less than 20 minutes. It looks even more delightful scattered with a few chopped pistachio nuts on top.

Serves 4-6.

Ingredients:

1 or 2 ripe Ogden, Galia or
   Charentais melons
175g (6oz) Parma ham cut into strips
1 tablespoon lemon juice

2½-3 tablespoons olive oil
1 tablespoon chopped mint
Freshly ground black pepper

Cut the melon in half and scoop out seeds. Peel and finely slice the flesh. Lay in a glass dish, alternating with strips of ham. Mix oil, lemon juice, mint and ground pepper. Leave to marinate at room temperature for at least an hour before serving.

SMOKED SALMON MOUSSE

This recipe is useful for using up small bits of smoked salmon you may have left over from making other dishes, or even sandwiches. I make it quite often in the summer months, and it works quite well with a small tin of red salmon.

Serves 4.

Ingredients:

1 large cup of smoked salmon bits
1 large cup of stiffly whipped
   double cream

Lemon juice
Aspic jelly
Paprika pepper

Purée salmon bits in a food mixer with a squeeze of lemon juice and a small teaspoonful of paprika. Lightly fold in an equal amount of stiffly whipped cream, and then add three tablespoons of liquid aspic jelly. Pour the mixture into a soufflé dish. Decorate the top with lemon rings and put in the fridge. When set, pour another layer of cool aspic over the top. Do this over the back of a tablespoon to prevent aspic from making a hole in the mixture and sinking to the bottom. Serve with crudités – radishes, cucumber or carrots.

TOMATO AND BASIL SOUP

The large beef tomatoes we can get in our greengrocers or supermarkets are ideal for this soup, and even on a warm day it tastes delicious served hot.

Serves 4.

Ingredients:

8 large beef tomatoes
2 tablespoons basil, finely chopped
600ml (1 pint) homemade chicken stock
  (or a chicken stock cube)
2 cloves garlic
240ml (8fl oz) double cream
Salt & pepper

Skin and remove pips from the tomatoes. Chop roughly and add garlic and simmer on hot plate for 20 minutes. Add stock and simmer for a further hour. Liquidize and put through a sieve. Taste and season with salt and pepper, and add the chopped basil. Place in a saucepan and heat up gently. Just before serving add cream, and adjust seasoning if necessary. Garnish with cream whirls and chopped basil. Serve with croutons or crusty rolls.

CREAMY ASPARAGUS SOUP

Asparagus can be quite expensive when it first arrives on the scene, so if I make this soup then it's usually when I have guests. Just double the quantity of ingredients if you are planning a dinner party for 6-8.

Serves 4.

Ingredients:

900g (2lb) asparagus
1 teaspoon caster sugar
1 litre (1¾ pints) vegetable stock
3 tablespoons white wine
2 egg yolks
50g (2oz) butter
Salt & pepper
1 tablespoon cornflour
Grated nutmeg
125ml (4fl oz) double cream

Wash and trim asparagus. Cook peelings with 25g (1oz) butter, and the sugar and salt in the stock for 20 minutes. Sieve, then discard the trimmings. Slice the asparagus at an angle. Melt remaining butter, add cornflour, and stir over moderate heat for 1 minute. Stir in stock, bring to the boil and add asparagus, and simmer for 10 minutes. Stir in the wine, season with nutmeg and pepper. Blend in a food processor or liquidiser until smooth. Return to pan. Whisk yolks and cream together, then whisk into soup. Heat gently. Sprinkle with parsley.

ASPARAGUS TART

You will find the ingredients in this recipe will make one large tart, but you can make small tartlets using the same ingredients and freezing the ones that are left over.

Serves 6.

Ingredients:

225g (8oz) shortcrust pastry	450g (1lb) fresh asparagus
1 small onion, peeled and chopped	10g (½oz) butter
300ml (½ pint) single cream	3 eggs
Pinch nutmeg	Salt & pepper
1 tablespoon grated Gruyere cheese	
(Cheddar will do just as well)	

Lightly scrape and trim asparagus. Place asparagus, lying flat, in a pan of boiling salted water for 10-12 minutes, or until tender. Drain, cut off and reserve tips, finely chop rest. Heat oven to 190C, 375F, Gas Mark 5. Melt butter over a low heat in frying pan, add onion and fry for 5 minutes to soften. Add chopped asparagus in the hot onion and butter. Roll out pastry on floured surface and line a 23cm (9 inch) pastry tin. Spoon mixture over base of pastry case and sprinkle with grated cheese. Lightly mix together eggs and cream, add nutmeg and season with salt and pepper. Pour mixture over asparagus and top with reserved tips. Place in centre of preheated oven and bake for 40 minutes, until set and pastry is crisp.

CIDER BAKED HADDOCK

In Somerset, where I spent most of my early growing up years, a generous dash of cider was put into most cooking, and a cider fruit cake was a great favourite in most families. I've used cider in this recipe, as it gives the fish a fresh, tangy taste and takes away the blandness.

Serves 4.

Ingredients:

700g (1½ lb) fresh haddock	1 egg, beaten
fillet, skinned	35g (1½oz) butter
Dry cider, enough to cover fish	35g (1½oz) flour
175g (6oz) grated Cheddar cheese	Salt & pepper
Milk	

Place haddock in a flat ovenproof dish. Add salt and pepper, and cover with cider. Seal dish with foil and bake in preheated oven 180C, 350F, Gas Mark 4 for 25-30 minutes, or until fish is cooked. Drain liquid and make up to 425ml (¾ pint) with milk. Cover fish with foil and keep warm. Make a sauce with the butter, flour and liquid. When cooked add 150g (5oz) of the cheese and continue cooking for 3 minutes. Remove sauce from heat and stir in the beaten egg. Pour sauce over fish and sprinkle remainder of cheese on top. Return to oven until cheese is melted and creamy on top.

PORK FILLETS IN GINGER WINE SAUCE

The amount of cream in this recipe may seem rather lavish, especially with pork, but it works well with the ginger wine and lemon, but make sure the pork fillets are nice and lean.

Serves 6-8.

Ingredients:

2 good sized pork fillets	75g (3oz) butter
2 small cartons double cream	Seasoned flour
Oil & lemon juice for marinade	12 tablespoons ginger wine
Salt & black pepper	Lemon slices and parsley

Slice the fillets and flatten them really thin. Marinate for 24 hours. Dip pork slices in the seasoned flour, and fry gently in heated butter in frying pan on both sides. Arrange slices on a dish and keep warm. **Sauce:** Add ginger wine to the pan and simmer until syrupy. Add cream and heat, but do not boil. Pour over the pork and garnish with lemon slices and chopped parsley.

HOT GAMMON

This dish is easy to cook and needs little preparation. If you are too busy to boil the gammon joint, soak it overnight, but be warned, it can be salty this way.

Serves 6-8.

Ingredients:

1.35kg (3lb) gammon joint	700g (1½lb) leeks
2 dessertspoons basil	1 dessertspoon pepper
1 dessertspoon sugar	450g-900g tin tomatoes

Bring gammon to the boil. Throw away water. Reboil and simmer for ¾ hour. Drain gammon and put into a deep casserole dish. Tip tomatoes and sliced leeks on top. Add basil, pepper and sugar, cover tightly and cook in a preheated oven 180C, 350F, Gas Mark 4 for about 1¼ hours, or until gammon is tender. Remove skin. Serve either whole or sliced with some of the juice and garnish with chopped parsley. Or you can thicken the remainder of the juice with a little cream and serve as a sauce. This joint will freeze, and is delicious eaten cold the next day with a crisp green salad.

EASY CHICKEN CASSEROLE

An easy meal to prepare when you have little or no time to spare, and it's a dish that will expand easily if you have a large number of guests to feed!

Serves 6.

Ingredients:

6 skinned chicken portions	1 red pepper, seeded & chopped
1 medium onion, peeled & chopped	1 clove garlic
1 tin condensed chicken or celery soup	

Chop garlic and add to chopped pepper and onion and put into a casserole dish. Place chicken portions on top. Mix the required amount of water to the soup and pour over the chicken. Season with pepper and salt. Cover casserole with foil or lid and cook in preheated oven 150C, 300F. Gas Mark 2 for 1½-2 hours. This dish can be prepared well in advance of when it is needed, but it will **not** freeze. Serve with vegetables of your choice.

PAN PIZZA

I call this dish my store cupboard standby! You can add cooked ham to the topping, or vary it by using mushrooms and tomatoes, in fact almost anything you have in your own store cupboard.

Serves 4-6.

Ingredients:

1 small onion	4 tablespoons cooking oil
1 400g (14oz) can tomatoes	1 level teaspoon oregano
Salt and pepper	175g (6oz) self-raising flour
60g (2½oz) hard margarine	1 teaspoon baking powder
5 tablespoons milk	50g (2oz) grated Cheddar cheese

Rub the margarine into the flour, add salt and baking powder. Mix to a smooth dough with the milk, and knead for a few minutes. Roll dough into a 25.5cm (10 inch) circle. Heat oil in a large frying pan, and fry the dough circle on a low heat for 4-5 minutes each side. Spread the tomatoes, spices and seasoning over the dough. Add the grated cheese and put under grill until the cheese has melted. Turn onto a warmed plate and cut into 4-6 wedges and serve with a crisp salad.

CURRIED CHICKEN TARTLETS

I usually make these into individual tartlets, but you can if you wish, make one large 20.5cm (8 inch tart), bake it longer at the lower temperature of 190C, 375F, Gas Mark 5. They are ideal to take on a picnic, placed in a rigid container for easy carrying.

Serves 4.

Ingredients:

175g (6oz) rich shortcrust pastry *(you can use bought pastry)*
350g (12oz) chicken meat, cut into thin strips
110g (4oz) walnuts *(roughly chopped)*

150ml (¼ pint) mayonnaise
2 teaspoons curry powder
Chopped fresh parsley
2 tablespoons lemon juice
Salt & pepper

Divide the pastry dough into four. Roll out each piece and use to line four 10cm (4 inch) diameter tartlet tins. Bake blind in preheated oven 200C, 400F, Gas Mark 6 for about 15 minutes, and allow to cool. Stir curry powder, lemon juice, walnuts and chicken into the mayonnaise, and add salt and pepper to taste. Spoon mixture into pastry cases and sprinkle with chopped parsley. Cover with cling film and store in fridge until the last possible moment before they are needed.

APPLE AND BANANA CRUMBLE

Using bananas in this apple crumble gives it an exotic flavour, and it's a good way of using up those bananas that always seem to get left in the fruit bowl.

Serves 6.

Ingredients:

900g (2lb) cooking apples, peeled & cored
2 ripe bananas
Sugar
1 small cup of sultanas
Pinch of cinnamon

Crumble:

110g (4oz) plain flour
75g (3oz) butter
50g (2oz) rolled oats
25g (1oz) ground almonds
35g (1½oz) caster sugar

Stew the apples gently in a little water with sugar to taste. Then place in a greased ovenproof dish with a layer of sliced banana, add the sultanas and cinnamon. Rub butter into flour until it resembles breadcrumbs, and then add ground almonds, oats and caster sugar. Cover the apple and banana with the crumble mixture and dot top with a little butter, and sprinkle over a little Demerara sugar. Bake in preheated oven 190C, 375F, Gas Mark 5 for approximately 30 minutes until crumble is golden brown and juices are beginning to bubble up through the topping.

HOT LEMON SOUFFLE

This is a delicious, light soufflé, which is particularly good after a rich main course. It can also be cooked using individual ramekin dishes, just bake it for a few minutes less than the time I have given in this recipe.

Serves 4.

Ingredients:
4 eggs   4 tablespoons caster sugar
Juice and rind of 1½ lemons

Beat egg yolks with sugar, grated lemon rind and juice for several minutes. Whip egg whites stiffly and fold into mixture. Pour into a buttered soufflé dish and cook for 10-12 minutes in preheated oven 180C, 350F, Gas Mark 4, until well risen and golden. Serve immediately.

RHUBARB AND RASPBERRY PIE

This is a colourful pie, with the rhubarb and raspberries giving a sharp fruity taste. It's good eaten hot or cold, served with single cream or homemade custard.

Serves 6-8.

Ingredients: For the pastry:
900g (2lb) rhubarb, wiped & trimmed   300g (10½oz) plain flour
110g (4oz) frozen raspberries   Pinch of salt
2 tablespoons of redcurrant jelly   75g (3oz) butter
3 tablespoons caster sugar   75g (3oz) lard
                                               5-6 tablespoons water

Cut rhubarb stalks into 2.5cm (1 inch) pieces. Put into a fairly large pan with the redcurrant jelly and gently stew over a very low heat until the juice begins to run from the rhubarb; then cook the rhubarb to a soft pulp. Stir in the raspberries and sugar and set aside to cool, making sure the fruit is completely cold when filling the pie. Sift flour with salt. Rub butter and lard into flour with tips of fingers. Mix the pastry to a firm consistency with the water. Cut off a third of the pastry for the lid. Roll out the remainder into a round an inch larger than a loose bottomed 23cm (9 inch) flan tin. Line flan tin with pastry, working it carefully into the base and up the sides of the tin. Fill pastry case with the cooled fruit and roll out the pastry for the top, making it a little larger than the tin. Moisten round the edge of the pastry already in the tin and cover the pie with the pastry lid. Press edges of pastry together and brush the top of the pie with lightly beaten egg white and sprinkle with caster sugar. Bake in preheated oven 190C, 375F, Gas Mark 5 for 40 minutes.

VIENNESE WHIRLS

These dainty little cakes are always popular at teatime. I sometimes fill them with lemon curd instead of jam, or make six of each. Be sure to keep them in an airtight tin before the jam is added.

Makes 12.

Ingredients:

225g (8oz) plain flour

225g (8oz) butter, softened

A few drops of vanilla essence

50g (2oz) caster sugar

Sifted icing sugar & raspberry jam

Put 12 paper cases on to a large baking sheet or into patty tins. Sift the flour and salt together into a bowl. Beat butter and caster sugar until light and creamy. Add the vanilla essence and half the sifted flour, and beat together. Add the remaining flour and beat again for a few minutes. Put the mixture into a piping bag fitted with a large star pipe and pipe it spirally into the paper cases, leaving a tiny hole in the middle. Bake in preheated oven 200C, 400F, Gas Mark 6 for about 10 minutes. The cakes will firm up after they have cooled. When cool, dredge the tops with icing sugar and fill the centres with raspberry jam or lemon curd.

CHOCOLATE TEA BISCUITS

When the cake tin is empty and I want to rustle up something quick for tea, then I make a batch of these biscuits. They are so easy to assemble in a food processor and they can be frozen.

Makes 24.

Ingredients:

110g (4oz) butter
50g (2oz) walnuts, chopped
110g (4oz) bar plain or milk
   chocolate, broken into pieces

110g (4oz) plain flour
110g (4oz) caster sugar

Process the butter and sugar in food mixer until pale and creamy. Add the broken pieces of chocolate and walnuts and process again in mixer. Add the flour and whiz again, making quite a stiff mixture. Roll into balls about the size of a walnut and place on a greased baking sheet a few inches apart. Flatten them down with a fork dipped in hot water and bake for about 10 minutes in preheated oven 190C, 375F, Gas Mark 5. Cool, and store in an airtight tin, as these biscuits tend to go a bit soggy.

SODA BREAD

Soda is a good alternative to yeast baked bread, I bake mine in my Aga (baking oven) for about 25 minutes, and serve it as soon as it is cooled from the oven.

Ingredients:

450g (1lb) plain flour
2 level teaspoons bicarbonate of soda
2 level teaspoons cream of tartar
300ml (½ pint) soured milk

1 teaspoon salt
25g (1oz) lard
1 teaspoon caster sugar

Sift dry ingredients into a large mixing bowl. Rub lard into the flour with fingertips until the mixture resembles fine breadcrumbs. Mix in the sugar. Make a well in the centre of the flour and add the milk (soured with 1 tablespoon of lemon juice) and mix to a firm dough. Turn dough on to a floured surface, knead it lightly and shape into a 18cm (7 inch) round, flatten and mark the round into four sections with the back of a knife. Put the loaf on to a floured baking tray and bake in the centre of a preheated oven 200C, 400F, Gas Mark 6 for about 30 minutes. Cool on wire tray.

ELDERFLOWER CHAMPAGNE

This is a refreshing, cool, summer drink, which is easy to make. The champagne won't keep like wine, but it will keep for 2-3 months, if you can keep it that long! Remember to pick the flowers when they are just out and not falling, otherwise it will make the champagne taste bitter.

Ingredients:

10 heads of elderflowers

2 tablespoons white wine vinegar

3.15 litres (8 pints) cold water

1 lemon

700g (1½lb) white sugar

Take off any green stems and pick over thoroughly. Put the blossoms into a bowl and sprinkle over the juice of the lemon. Grate the lemon rind and add this along with the sugar and vinegar. Add the cold water and leave for 24 hours. Strain into bottles, cork firmly, and lay the bottles on their sides. Do not disturb for two weeks, when the champagne should be sparkling and ready to drink.

Contents – June

June

*T*his month brings the warmer weather, with the lighter nights and being able to sit outside to eat meals with family and friends. It's the month for salads, with many varieties of lettuce and plenty of tomatoes, cucumbers, watercress and spring onions. It's a busy month for the housewife too, with all the summer fruits that burst on the scene. English strawberries are at their best in June, and with a sprinkling of sugar and plenty of cream, one of the easiest of desserts to serve. I like to make my jams and jellies this month – strawberry and gooseberry, and the early raspberries and redcurrants are usually ripe by the end of the month.

And with a little preparation we can take the heat out of the kitchen by cooking dishes well in advance, such as cold soups, meats, flans and pies, which can all be stored in the fridge or freezer until needed.

WATERCRESS SOUP

This is what I call a dainty soup as opposed to a chunky one, and it's just right for summer. You can, if you wish, serve it chilled, but I like it best hot, even on a summer's day!

Serves 3-4.

Ingredients:

1 bunch of watercress, chopped finely
1 medium onion, peeled & sliced
2 good sized potatoes, peeled & sliced
Salt & pepper

150ml (¼ pint) milk
300ml (½ pint) chicken stock
  (stock cube will do)

Cook sliced potatoes and onions in stock. Then pass through a sieve or liquidizer. Return to saucepan with milk, seasoning and watercress. Simmer for about 10 minutes until soup is reheated, but do not boil. Serve immediately.

COURGETTE VINAIGRETTE

I make this courgette vinaigrette time and again during the summer months, sometimes adding a sliced red pepper to give the dish extra colour.

Serves 4.

Ingredients:

1 onion or 3 shallots, peeled & chopped
Strips of peeled, seeded tomato
  for garnish
12 even sized courgettes
  (*I usually allow 3 per person*)

Olive oil
Vinaigrette dressing
Salt & pepper

Blanch courgettes for 2 minutes in boiling water. Drain well. Heat olive oil in large pan, sauté onion until transparent. Slice courgettes and add to pan together with salt and pepper, and sauté gently until just tender. Put into a bowl and whilst still warm, toss in vinaigrette dressing. Chill before serving.

SALMON PIE

This dish is very simple to prepare and makes a special main course for summer entertaining. The cucumber sauce is a perfect accompaniment, and can be made well in advance and put in the fridge until needed.

Serves 4.

Ingredients:
450g (1lb) fresh or tinned salmon)
4 eggs (2 hardboiled)
50g (2oz) butter
2 teaspoons chopped parsley
¼ teaspoon salt
¼ teaspoon sweet basil

Cucumber Sauce:
1 medium cucumber
1 small onion sliced
2 teaspoons vinegar
½ cup thick soured cream
2 teaspoons chopped parsley,
  salt & pepper
2 dessertspoons mayonnaise or
  salad cream

Line a 20.5cm (8 inch) round baking tin or quiche dish with shortcrust pastry. Slice the two hard-boiled eggs, and arrange into the bottom of the pastry shell. Flake the fresh or tinned salmon into a bowl, removing skin and bones. Add the remaining two eggs, beaten, together with all the remaining ingredients and the melted butter, then pour the mixture over the salmon and bake in preheated oven 220C, 425F, Gas Mark 7 for 25 minutes. Serve hot with the cucumber sauce.
To make sauce: Grate cucumber and finely chop sliced onion. Add the 2 dessertspoons of mayonnaise together with the remaining ingredients, salt and pepper to taste and mix thoroughly. Serve sauce separately.

SPICY CHICKEN BREASTS

The combination of garlic and ginger gives this dish an oriental flavour, and it doesn't take long to prepare and cook.

Serves 4.

Ingredients:
4 chicken breasts, skinned
3 tablespoons clear honey
1 teaspoon ground ginger
½ teaspoon black pepper

75g (3oz) butter
3 cloves garlic, crushed
½ teaspoon salt
3 tablespoons sesame seeds

Melt butter in a large frying pan over a moderate heat, when foam subsides, add the honey and stir constantly. Add garlic, ginger, salt and pepper. Increase the heat to high and fry chicken breasts for 5 minutes on each side or until the chicken breasts are golden brown all over. Transfer the chicken to an ovenproof baking dish and sprinkle over the sesame seeds. Pour over the juices and place the dish in preheated oven 200C, 400F, Gas Mark 6 for 25-30 minutes or until the chicken is tender and the juices run clear when it is pierced with the point of a sharp knife. Remove dish from the oven and serve immediately. Serve with buttered noodles sprinkled with oregano and a bottle of well-chilled dry white wine.

ROAST LAMB WITH MINTY BALL STUFFING

Ask your butcher to bone your joint of lamb, which will make it easier to carve and serve, and if you dislike the taste of mint, then try glazing the lamb with 3 tablespoons of redcurrant jelly brushed over the joint 25 minutes before the end of cooking time.

Serves 4-6.

Ingredients:	For the stuffing:
1.15kg (2½lb) lean lamb leg or shoulder	1 onion, peeled & chopped
2 cloves garlic, sliced	1 garlic clove, crushed
8-10 fresh mint leaves	1 teaspoon oil
	110g (4oz) dry breadcrumbs
	2 tablespoons mint jelly
	1 teaspoon fresh mint, chopped

Cut slits into the joint and push in the slithers of garlic and mint leaves. Place the joint on a rack in a roasting tin and roast in preheated oven 180C, 350F, Gas Mark 4, allowing 25 minutes per 450g (1lb) plus 25 minutes over, a little longer if you want your joint well done. Meanwhile make the stuffing: fry the onion and garlic in the oil for 3-4 minutes until soft. Stir in the remaining ingredients and mix. Shape into 6-8 stuffing balls. Place on a baking tray and bake for the last 20 minutes of cooking time. Serve the joint with the stuffing, roast potatoes, carrots and broccoli.

BEEF BURGERS

If you are feeling energetic it's a good idea to make a batch of these burgers, they freeze well and if you have hungry children to feed you will find it useful to have some handy in your freezer. The BBQ sauce can be served hot or cold with the burgers, and adds a tasty filling.

Makes 4-6.

Ingredients:
450g (1lb) lean minced beef
2 tablespoons tomato sauce
1 tablespoon Worcestershire sauce
Salt & black pepper

BBQ Sauce:
5 tablespoons tomato ketchup
2 tablespoons Worcestershire sauce
½ teaspoon English Mustard
1 clove garlic, crushed

Place all the beef burger ingredients into a large bowl and mix thoroughly. Divide the mixture into 4 or 6 and shape into burgers. Place under a preheated grill for 4-6 minutes each side, until cooked thoroughly, turning once.
To make BBQ Sauce: Mix all the ingredients for the sauce together and serve hot or cold. Serve the burgers with a large bread bun, salad and BBQ sauce.

LAMB AND LENTIL CURRY

You can use beef or pork in this recipe, but lamb and curry go well together and you can use either shoulder or leg – ask your butcher to cube it for you.

Serves 4-6.

Ingredients:
900g (2lb) lean lamb, cubed
2 x 400g (14oz) cans chopped tomatoes
2 medium onions, peeled & chopped
2 red peppers, seeded &
  cut into chunks
225g (8oz) cauliflower,
  cut into small florets

600ml (1 pint) stock
110g (4oz) red or green lentils
2 cloves of garlic, crushed
3 tablespoons curry paste
2 tablespoons tomato purée

In a large casserole dish place all the ingredients except the cauliflower and red peppers. Mix well, cover and place in a preheated oven 170C, 325F, Gas Mark 3 for 1-1½ hours until meat is tender. Stir in the cauliflower and red peppers, and return to the oven for a further 30 minutes. Serve with rice, seasonal vegetables and chutneys.

STRAWBERRY ICE-CREAM

This recipe makes a little fruit go a long way – best made the day before you are going to eat it.

Serves 4.

Ingredients:

225g (8oz) strawberries
Squeeze of lemon juice
Garnish with 6-8 large
  sliced strawberries

75g (3oz) icing sugar
150ml (¼ pint) double cream
150ml (¼ pint) single cream

Hull and lightly wash strawberries in a colander, drain them thoroughly and cut them into small pieces. Put them in a liquidiser, with the sieved sugar and lemon juice, or alternatively, rub the strawberries through a fine sieve and add the sugar and lemon juice to the purée. Whisk the two creams until thick, but not stiff, and blend this well into the strawberry purée. Spoon the strawberry mixture into a plastic freezing container, cover with a lid and leave to freeze for 12 hours. One or two hours before serving, remove the ice cream from the freezing compartment and thaw slightly in the refrigerator. Scoop the ice cream into individual glasses and decorate with slices of fresh strawberries. Will freeze for up to 3 months.

RASPBERRY DELIGHT

This is just the pudding to make on a hot summer's day, when you want to be out in the garden enjoying the sunshine. It's easy to make and needs no cooking.

Serves 4.

Ingredients:

225g (8oz) raspberries
225g (8oz) cream cheese

1 x 150ml (¼ pint) carton soured cream
1 x 150ml (¼ pint) natural yoghurt

Put the cream cheese through a fine sieve and blend in the yoghurt and soured cream, or you can mix them together in a blender. Spoon into a shallow serving dish, or you can use 4 individual ones, smooth over the top with a knife and leave to chill. Just before serving, pile the prepared raspberries on top. A little caster sugar sprinkled over the raspberries gives the dish an inviting effect and it tastes sweeter.

BAKED LEMON SURPRISE SPONGE

A delicious sponge pudding with a surprise layer of lemon sauce at the bottom.

Serves 6-8.

Ingredients:
175g (6oz) self-raising flour
175g (6oz) soft margarine
175g (6oz) caster sugar
3 eggs, beaten
Grated rind of 2 lemons

Sauce:
175g (6oz) caster sugar
2 dessertspoons cornflour
Juice of 2 lemons made up to
    425ml (¾ pint) with hot water

Whisk all the sponge ingredients together until pale and fluffy, adding a little milk if too stiff. Place mixture in a deep greased dish, making sure there is enough room for the sauce. Mix sugar and cornflour together and add hot water/lemon juice, stir well and pour over the uncooked sponge mixture. Bake in preheated oven 180C, 350F, Gas Mark 4 for 1-1½ hours when sponge has risen and is golden.

PINEAPPLE MERINGUE PUDDING

I've used pineapple in this recipe, but with the arrival of all the summer fruits this month there is a wide variety of choice, and gooseberries and apricots make ideal alternatives.

Serves 4-6.

Ingredients:
1 small tin of pineapple
50g (2oz) margarine
50g (2oz) flour
2 egg yolks for the base
35g (1½oz) granulated sugar
The juice of a large tin of pineapple
    made up to 300ml (½ pint) with milk

For the meringue:
4 egg whites
50g (2oz) caster sugar
50g (2oz) granulated sugar

To make the pudding, melt the margarine in a saucepan. Remove from the heat and stir in the flour. Then gradually add the milk and juice mixture making a sauce. Return to the heat and bring to the boil, stirring continually until the mixture is thick. Stir in the granulated sugar and the yolks from the two eggs. Chop the pineapple and add to the mixture. Pour into a greased shallow pie dish and cook in preheated oven 180C, 350F, Gas Mark 4 for 20 minutes until set. To make the meringue: Whisk the four egg whites. Fold in the caster sugar and the granulated sugar. Pile on top of the pudding. Sprinkle a little caster sugar on top for crispness. Turn the temperature up to 190C, 375F, Gas Mark 5 and cook pudding for a further 10-15 minutes so that the meringue is crisp and golden brown.

73

FRUITY OAT BARS

These fruity bars are excellent for lunch boxes or picnics, and are popular with children. They freeze well too.

Makes 12-15 bars.

Ingredients:

175g (6oz) butter
175g (6oz) wholemeal self-raising flour
25g (1oz) chopped peel
35g (1½oz) sunflower seeds
10g (½oz) extra sunflower seeds

175g (6oz) soft brown sugar
200g (7oz) mixed dried fruit
50g (2oz) porridge oats
2 eggs, lightly beaten

Melt the butter and sugar over a gentle heat in a large saucepan. Add flour, fruit, oats and 35g (1½oz) sunflower seeds and lightly beaten eggs, and mix well. Spread the mixture evenly in the tin, and sprinkle with the extra 10g (½oz) sunflower seeds. Bake in preheated oven 170C, 325F, Gas Mark 3 for about 40-45 minutes. Cool in tin, then cut into bars.

LEMON CURD CAKE

This is a "knock-up quick" cake, which can be made in virtually a few minutes. I often serve it as a pudding with a dollop of cream.

Serve 6.

Ingredients:

110g (4oz) caster sugar
225g (8oz) self-raising flour
4 eggs, beaten

175g (6oz) soft margarine
4 tablespoons lemon curd

Cream together the sugar and margarine, add the lemon curd and beaten eggs. Fold in the flour and put into a greased 900g (2 lb) loaf tin and bake in preheated oven at 180C, 350F, Gas Mark 4 for approximately 1-1½ hours until risen and golden brown. Cool in tin for a few minutes before turning out on rack.

CHOCOLATE COCONUT BUNS

These little buns are old time favourites, and they are a great success at children's parties and disappear like hot cakes at local bazaars and fetes. For special occasions or tea parties, melt a little chocolate and spread on top of the buns.

Makes about 18-20.

Ingredients:

110g 4oz) butter
2 eggs, beaten
110g (4oz) desiccated coconut
2 tablespoons milk

110g (4oz) caster sugar
110g (4oz) self-raising flour
110g (4oz) chocolate drops

Cream the butter with the sugar until pale and fluffy. Beat in the eggs, add a little of the flour to prevent curdling. Fold in the remaining flour, coconut and chocolate drops. Then fold in milk to soften the mixture. Divide between 20 greased patty tins and bake in a preheated oven 180C, 350F. Gas Mark 4 for about 15-20 minutes until risen and golden. Turn out and cool on wire rack.

CHEESE AND VEGETABLE PASTIES

Traditionally Pasties are filled with meat and potatoes, but these Cheese and Vegetable Pasties make a nice change, and they are delicious eaten hot or cold for lunch with a salad, and ideal to take on picnics.

Serves 4-6.

Ingredients:

350g (12oz) shortcrust pastry
1 carrot, scraped, cooked & diced
Seasoning
350g (12oz) mixed root vegetables,
  peeled, cooked & diced

225g (8oz) Cheddar cheese, diced
½ teaspoon mixed herbs
1 egg, beaten
Watercress

Roll out pastry and cut out six saucer-sized circles. Mix together vegetables, cheese, herbs and seasoning. Divide between pastry circles, damp edges of pastry and draw together, pinch with fingers to seal edges. Place on a baking sheet, brush with egg and bake at 200C, 400F, Gas Mark 6 for 25 minutes, until golden brown.

SAUSAGE PIZZA

I think homemade pizzas beat the commercially bought ones hands down. The variations of toppings and fillings are endless, and you can prepare some scone bases in advance and freeze them until you need them.

Serves 6.

Ingredients:
2 medium onions
10g (½oz) margarine
½ level teaspoon mixed dried herbs
Salt & pepper
110g (4oz) Cheddar cheese

Scone Base:
225g (8oz) plain flour
50g (2oz) margarine
7 tablespoons of milk
225g (8oz) pork & beef chipolatas
Tomatoes & parsley

Preheat oven to 200C, 400F, Gas Mark 6. Brush baking sheet with oil. Peel and finely chop onion and melt the 10g (½oz) margarine in a medium sized saucepan over a fairly low heat. Add onions, herbs, salt and pepper and cook until onions are tender. Grate cheese coarsely. To make scone base: Put flour into a large mixing bowl and run margarine into the flour with tips of fingers. Add the 7 tablespoons of milk and mix thoroughly bringing the mixture together and kneading gently into a ball. Put pastry onto a floured surface and roll out into a 23cm (9 inch) circle and place on baking sheet. Spread onion mixture over scone base to cover. Sprinkle cheese over onion mixture, and arrange sausages on top. Bake in oven for 30-35 minutes. Place on a serving dish, cut tomatoes in wedges and put between sausages. Put a sprig of parsley in centre. Serve hot or cold with vegetables or a green salad.

RASPBERRY GIN

This is a good way of using up raspberries, and you don't have to throw them away, just put them in a summer trifle, you'll find they will give it a very potent flavour!

Ingredients:
1.8kg (4lb) raspberries
900g (2lb) caster sugar

1½ litres (2 pints) gin

Hull the fruit and put into a large jar. Add the gin and sugar and cover the top of the jar with kitchen foil. Stir often during the first week to be sure that it has dissolved. Leave for 6 months. Strain and bottle.

MOCK CREAM

I very often make this mock cream to fill sponges. This quantity is sufficient to fill 3 Victoria Sponges, and will freeze divided into 3 and put into cartons.

Ingredients:
225g (8oz) unsalted butter   50g (2oz) icing sugar
1 teaspoon boiling water   ½ small tin evaporated milk
Vanilla essence to taste

Cream butter and sugar together until light and creamy. Add 1 teaspoon boiling water and beat well again. Add evaporated milk, a little at a time, and at the same time add the vanilla essence. Beat for another 2 to 3 minutes. You should now have a light creamy filling.

STRAWBERRY JAM

If you live near a PYO fruit farm, pick your fruit early in the morning before the heat of the day gets on the strawberries, but if you grow your own, then there's nothing better.

Yields 2¼ kg (5 lb)

Ingredients:
1.6kg (3½lb) strawberries, hulled   1.35kg (3lb) sugar
The juice of one large lemon

Heat the strawberries and lemon juice gently in a preserving pan or large saucepan, stirring to reduce the volume. Add the sugar and stir until dissolved. Boil until setting point is reached (at this stage you can add extra lemon juice if the jam is taking awhile to set). Skim any scum off and set the jam aside for a while to allow the fruit to sink (about 15 minutes). Stir gently to distribute the strawberries. Pour into warm, dry jars and cover immediately with waxed covers.

Contents – July

July

*T*his is the month for barbecues and supper parties, which can be a delight in summer when meals can be enjoyed outdoors in the still, warm evenings. And it's a month for variety, when we have simple salads where you can choose from the basic green leaf to a colourful array of herbs, rocket and watercress. July usually sees a drop in prices, with fruit in plentiful supply to use in main dishes and salads as well as desserts, and the glorious soft fruit season arrives with the really hot weather.

Gooseberries and strawberries are joined by red and blackcurrants to use in mousses and fools, which make delicious desserts just right for the height of the summer. It's a month to enjoy and savour all it has to offer whether indoors or outdoors, and my recipes in this chapter will help you plan that special dinner or supper party all with a hint of a 'Taste of Summer'.

BLACK PEPPERCORN MARINADE

I think marinades are important to whatever is being barbecued, and well worth a little time and effort in preparing them. This marinade is suitable for steaks, sausages, chicken and lamb, and you can make it well in advance of your barbecue party, giving you extra time to do other things.

Ingredients:

1 tablespoon chopped parsley

2 tablespoons coarsely crushed
   black peppercorns

2-3 tablespoons lemon juice

1 clove garlic, crushed

Combine all the ingredients in a bowl. Mix well and place meat or sausages in the mixture, stirring to coat. Cover and leave for at least an hour, then cook on your barbecue.

BARBECUED PORK

This is a strongly flavoured meal, so make sure you serve a robust wine with it. An Australian Chardonnay or a Cabernet Sauvignon would be ideal.

Serves 4.

Ingredients:

1 medium sized tenderloin of pork

3 tablespoons olive or cooking oil

6 large cloves of garlic

6 tablespoons soy sauce

Mix the soy sauce and olive oil in a bowl large enough to take all of the meat. Crush the garlic clove and add to the sauce and oil. Stir vigorously. Cut the meat into eight equal pieces and flatten slightly with a meat mallet or rolling pin. Give the liquid another stir and add the meat. Leave the meat to marinate for as long as possible, but not for less than two hours. Cook on a very hot barbecue until the juices run clear when the meat is pricked with a skewer. Use the excess marinade as a baste. After the juices run clear, cook for two more minutes and serve piping hot with a mixed salad containing plenty of onions and pepper.

GRAPEFRUIT JELLY MOULD

This jelly mould goes well with cold meats and flans, and keeps for 4 days in the fridge.

Ingredients:

1 medium tin grapefruit segments
1 tablespoon freshly chopped mint
  (or teaspoon mint sauce)

1 packet lime jelly
1 tablespoon cider vinegar
850ml (1½ pint) ring mould

Drain juice from grapefruit. Melt jelly in 300ml (½ pint) hot water. Make up grapefruit juice and vinegar to 300ml (½ pint), then stir in dissolved jelly and grapefruit segments and mint. Pour into mould and leave to set. For a special dinner party fill the centre with prawns in a yoghurt dressing, sprinkled with chopped chives.

GREEK SALAD

A cool, crisp salad, which makes a perfect starter or a light lunch for a hot summer's day. Feta cheese is used in this recipe, but a crumbly white British cheese, such as Caerphilly or Wensleydale tastes just as good.

Serves 4.

Ingredients:
½ cucumber
4 tomatoes
1 green pepper
1 onion
225g (8oz) feta cheese
12 black olives

Dressing:
3 tablespoons olive oil
Salt & pepper to taste
1 tablespoon white wine vinegar

Cut cucumber into 5cm (2 inch) sticks. Quarter tomatoes, seed and slice green pepper, peel and slice onion and arrange in salad bowl. Whisk oil and seasoning together, pour over salad and toss gently to coat. Slice or crumble the feta cheese and sprinkle over salad. Garnish with black olives.

PRAWN TOMATO MOULDS

These moulds can be eaten as a very light lunch with a salad, or as a starter.

Serves 4.

Ingredients:

600ml (1 pint) tomato juice
4 minced cocktail gherkins
Few drops Tabasco sauce
Salt & Pepper

150g (5oz) peeled prawns
10g (½ oz) gelatine
2 teaspoons lemon juice

Dissolve the gelatine in minimum amount of water and mix thoroughly with rest of ingredients. Put mixture into 4 individual moulds and leave to set. Turn out moulds on beds of lettuce and decorate each with a prawn and fresh mayonnaise.

CALVES LIVER PATÉ

Some crusty rolls or bread and a crisp salad with paté, makes a quick satisfying lunch on a summer's day when you don't want to spend time inside cooking.

Serves 4.

Ingredients:

350g (12ozs) calves liver, sliced
1 clove garlic
175g (6ozs) streaky bacon, chopped
5 anchovy fillets (optional)
300ml (½ pint) white sauce

1 small onion
25g (1oz) butter
1 egg, beaten
1 dessertspoon brandy
Salt & pepper

Heat butter in pan and sauté sliced liver, sliced onion and chopped garlic for about 5 minutes. Then put through a fine mincer or food processor with chopped bacon and anchovies, reserving a few bacon rashers to line tin. Season and beat in white sauce, egg and brandy. Put into tin or mould lined with bacon, cover and cook in preheated oven 180C, 350F, Gas Mark 4 for 1-1½ hours.

CUCUMBER AU GRATIN

There should be plenty of cucumbers about this month and they can be used in many ways other than in salads. This gratin makes a versatile alternative.

Serves 4-6.

Ingredients:

2 cucumbers, peeled
175g (6ozs) Cheddar cheese
A little chopped parsley

50g (2ozs) butter
Salt & pepper

Cut cucumbers into 8cm (3 inch) pieces, and slice each piece in half, lengthways, remove seeds. Cook the cucumber in boiling, salted water for 6 minutes, drain and dry. Butter an oven proof dish and arrange a layer of cucumber in the base of the dish, sprinkle with a third of the cheese and season with salt and pepper. Repeat these layers finishing with cheese and dot with butter, and sprinkle with chopped parsley. Bake in centre of preheated oven at 200C, 400F, Gas Mark 6 for 30 minutes until bubbly and golden brown. Serve as a side dish with meats or fish.

SALMON AND COURGETTES WITH CREAMY PASTA

This makes a perfect summer's evening meal, especially if you are entertaining. If you are inviting more than 4 guests just double up on the quantity of ingredients.

Serves 4.

Ingredients:

300g (10½ozs) salmon tail off-cuts
1 small onion, finely chopped
2 courgettes, washed & cut into
  bite-sized chunks

1 tablespoon olive oil or butter
110g (4oz) pasta shapes
1 x 200g (7oz) crème fraiche
Salt & freshly ground black pepper

Lightly poach or steam salmon pieces for 5 minutes. Leave to cool, remove any bones, and keep the fish in bite-sized pieces. Cook pasta according to directions. Drain. Heat oil or butter in a large pan, and cook onion until softened. Add courgette pieces and continue to cook for about 5 minutes. Add cooked salmon and pasta, stir, add créme fraiche, season well with freshly ground black pepper, and salt to taste.

MACKEREL PARCELS WITH GOOSEBERRY SAUCE

It's always best to buy mackerel fairly small, nowadays they are mostly boned and ready for you to cook, if not, your fishmonger will bone them for you. And if you're not too keen on gooseberries, try a purée of rhubarb instead, with a little sugar added to take the sharpness off.

Serves 4.

Ingredients:
4 medium sized mackerel, cleaned
Black pepper & salt
Slices of lemon
Chopped parsley
Lightly greased foil

Gooseberry Sauce:
225g (8oz) gooseberries
Sugar to taste
A little water

Cut 4 pieces of kitchen foil large enough to wrap up each fish. Season the fish well. Lightly grease the foil and put one mackerel on each piece. Arrange the lemon slices on the fish, and sprinkle with parsley. Twist the ends of the foil. Put the parcels on a greased baking tin and cook in preheated oven 190C, 375F, Gas Mark 5 and bake for 20-25 minutes. To make sauce: Top and tail gooseberries and wash them well. Put fruit into saucepan, add a little water and cook until they soften, then sweeten to taste. Rub through a sieve or liquidise. The sauce should be sharp and tangy.

BACON AND EGG PIE

A perennial favourite for picnic and summer meals, full of savoury aromas and tastes, and can be eaten hot or cold.

Serves 4-6.

Ingredients:
225g (8oz) shortcrust pastry
1 large onion, sliced
120g (4½oz) streaky bacon,
   cut into small strips
50g (2oz) Cheddar cheese, grated
Salt & pepper

25g (1oz) butter
1 tomato sliced
Squeeze of lemon juice
4-5 eggs
Milk to glaze

Use two-thirds of pastry to line a 20.5cm (8 inch) greased pie plate, and bake blind in centre of a preheated oven 180C, 350F, Gas Mark 4 for 10-15 minutes. Melt butter in a pan and fry bacon, remove and then fry onion. Arrange bacon on the bottom of cooked pastry case and cover with onion. Add tomato slices, salt and pepper and lemon juice. Break the eggs on top and sprinkle with grated cheese.

Roll out the remaining pastry and use to cover the pie. Flute edges and make a centre leaf decoration with pastry trimmings. Brush with milk and bake in centre of oven for 35-40 minutes.

POTATO SALAD

Waxy new potatoes coated with a mayonnaise dressing, chives, spring onions and leeks make a dish that can almost be eaten on it's own, in fact I often do!

Serves 4.

Ingredients:

450g (1lb) waxy new potatoes
  (cooked & sliced)
1 tablespoon olive oil
1 tablespoon lemon juice
2 tablespoons chopped spring onions

110g (4oz) mayonnaise
2 tablespoons chopped chives
4 tablespoons chopped leeks
Salt & pepper to taste

Place the potatoes in a mixing bowl. Combine together mayonnaise, lemon juice, oil, salt and pepper, spring onions and 1 tablespoon chopped chives. Add to the potatoes and toss gently until they are well coated. Spoon the mixture into a serving bowl, sprinkle with remaining chives and scatter chopped leeks around the edge of the bowl. Cover and chill for 30 minutes before serving.

MELON AND PRAWN SALAD

I often make this salad in July when shellfish is at its best. If you double up on the ingredients it makes a cool and refreshing summer's day lunch, without too much effort to prepare.

Serves 4.

Ingredients:

1 Honeydew melon
  (halved, deseeded & cubed)
175g (6oz) peeled prawns
1 tablespoon grated lemon rind
Salt & freshly ground black pepper

2 tablespoons tomato purée
1 teaspoon castor sugar
200ml (⅓ pint) mayonnaise
Lettuce Leaves

Mix melon pieces and peeled prawns together. Mix together mayonnaise, tomato purée, lemon rind, sugar, salt and pepper to taste, and then add the melon and prawn mixture, stir gently. Arrange lettuce leaves on a serving dish and pile the prawn and melon mixture in the centre, or arrange on 4 individual dishes. Garnish with watercress and a few whole prawns.

FOUR BERRY JELLY

A colourful, jewelled berry dessert, guaranteed to enhance any dinner or supper party you give this month.

Serves 4-6.

Ingredients:

110g (4oz) raspberries, hulled   110g (4oz) strawberries, hulled
50g (2oz) redcurrants, stalks removed   300ml (½ pint) red wine
50g (2oz) blackcurrants, stalks removed   300ml (½ pint) grape juice
75g (3oz) caster sugar   10g (½oz) gelatine

Put the red wine in a saucepan with the sugar and heat gently to dissolve. Remove from heat and allow to cool. Stir in the grape juice. Dissolve the gelatine in 6 tablespoons hot water, stir into the red wine mixture and pour into an 850ml (1½ pint) loaf tin and put into fridge to set. Mix the raspberries, redcurrants and blackcurrants together, slice strawberries and gently mix in with the other fruit. When jelly begins to set, about 40 minutes, add fruit, distributing evenly through the jelly. Return to fridge and leave for 4-5 hours. To serve, run a knife around the inner edge of tin and invert jelly onto a plate. Cut into thick slices and serve with cream or ice cream.

GOOSEBERRY PIE

I think the name says it all, and I was almost tempted to add 'with custard'. Years ago gooseberry pie, like apple pie, was a traditional pudding after the Sunday main roast meal, it's a pie I never tire of, and I make it often when the gooseberries are around.

Serves 4-6.

Ingredients: Filling:
175g (6oz) plain flour   750g (1½lb) gooseberries, topped & tailed
75g (3oz) butter, diced   175g (6oz) caster sugar
25g (1oz) caster sugar
Pinch of salt
1 egg yolk
2 tablespoons cold water

Sift flour with salt and sugar into a large mixing bowl. Add diced butter and rub into the flour until the mixture resembles fine breadcrumbs. Add the beaten egg yolk, and then the 2 tablespoons of water and mix to a fairly stiff dough. Wrap in cling film and chill for 30 minutes. Roll out pastry on a lightly floured surface to a round 4cm (1½ inches) larger than a 850ml (1½ pint) ovenproof dish. Cut off strip round the edges. Mix gooseberries with caster sugar and spoon into pie dish. Dampen rim of the dish with water and place the pastry strip on the rim. Brush pastry strip with egg. Place the pastry lid on top of dish and press round edges to seal properly. Trim surplus dough and crimp edge of pie. Brush lid with egg and sprinkle with caster sugar. Make a couple of slits in the lid to let the steam escape. Bake pie in preheated oven 200C, 400F, Gas Mark 6 for about 30 minutes, until the crust is crisp and golden. Sprinkle with caster sugar and serve the pie hot with custard or cream.

TRADITIONAL SUMMER PUDDING

This is one of my favourite puddings, and I try to make it at least two or three times during the summer fruit season.

Serves 4-6.

Ingredients:
700g (1½lb) soft red fruit (raspberries, black & red currants, etc.)
110g (4oz) caster sugar (extra if you have a sweet tooth!)
8 slices of day-old white bread, with crusts removed
Strip of lemon rind

Put the fruit into a bowl with sugar to taste, and add the lemon rind. Leave overnight. Turn the fruit into a pan, discard lemon rind and simmer for 3 minutes, until very lightly cooked. Remove from heat. Cut a circle from one slice of bread to fit the bottom of a 1½ litre (2 pint) pudding basin. Line the base and sides of the basin with bread, filling in any gaps with small pieces of bread. Then fill with the fruit and juices from cooking. Cover with bread slices. Place a flat plate and a 900g (2lb) weight on top, and leave overnight in fridge. Turn out onto a plate and serve with whipped cream.

STRAWBERRY CHEESECAKE

This is just the dessert to round off a summer lunch or dinner – it freezes well too.

Serves 6.

Ingredients:

Strawberry jam
Juice and rind of 1 lemon
Few drops of vanilla essence
225g (8oz) strawberries
10g (½oz) gelatine dissolved in
   2-3 tablespoons water
Base:
175g (6oz) finely crushed digestive
   biscuits, mixed with 75g (3oz)
   melted butter.

350g (12oz) cream cheese
110g (4oz) caster sugar
2 eggs separated
300ml (½ pint) whipped cream

Press the base into a 20.5-23 cm (8-9 inch) spring sided tin. Liquidise cheese, lemon juice and rind, sugar, vanilla essence, egg yolks and gelatine. Divide mixture in two. To one half add half the strawberries, crushed. To the other, fold in the cream. Whisk egg whites and fold half into each mixture. Spoon strawberry mixture over base, and top with plain mixture. Chill. Remove from tin (freeze at this point if required). Serve topped with remaining strawberries, thinly sliced and glazed with a little warmed strawberry jam.

RASPBERRY WALNUT SLICES

I recently came across this recipe in one of my daughter's old school cookery books, and it has since become a firm family tea-time favourite.

Makes 12 slices.

Ingredients:

50g (2oz) butter
Yolk of 1 egg
Raspberry jam

75g (3oz) caster sugar
75g (3oz) plain flour
50g (2oz) chopped walnuts

Cream the butter and sugar, then add egg yolk and flour making a stiff dough. Roll out the dough on a floured surface to fit a greased and lined Swiss roll tin 25.5cm x 20.5cm (10 x 8 inches) . Prick well and bake in preheated oven 200C, 400F, Gas Mark 6 for 10 minutes, then spread a thin layer of raspberry jam on top. Whisk egg white stiffly with 75g (3 oz) caster sugar and spread over jam and top with the chopped walnuts. Return to oven and bake at the lower heat of 180C, 350F, Gas Mark 4 for about 15 minutes. When cool cut into 12 slices.

RASPBERRY TARTLETS

These dainty little tartlets can be made using any fruit of your choice, but I think raspberries sit comfortably in the pastry cases covered with a shiny redcurrant glaze.

Makes about 12-15.

Ingredients:

175g (6oz) rich shortcrust pastry
110g (4oz) redcurrant jelly

225-250g (8oz-9oz) raspberries
225g (8oz) cream cheese

Roll out prepared pastry thinly and with a cutter cut into 5cm (2 inch) rounds. Bake blind for about 8 minutes at 190C, 375F, Gas Mark 5. When they are golden brown take from the oven and cool on wire tray. Add sugar to taste to the cream cheese, if a little too dry, add enough cream to moisten it. When tartlet cases are cold, fill with cream cheese and arrange the raspberries on top. Beat redcurrant jelly until smooth and heat it just a little. Brush this over the raspberries. Well worth a little time and effort to get a really professional result.

STRAWBERRY & CREAM SPONGE

If you aren't counting calories this sponge can be served slightly warm as a pudding, with a dollop of crème fraiche!

Serves 6-8.

Ingredients:

110g (4oz) self-raising flour
4 large eggs
70ml (2½ fl oz) oil

25g (1oz) cornflour
175g (6oz) caster sugar
¼ teaspoon vanilla essence

Whisk eggs and caster sugar together in a large bowl until thick and creamy, leaving a trail when beaters are lifted. Gently pour the oil, a little at a time, down the sides of the bowl. Sift flour and cornflour together and fold into beaten mixture, add the vanilla essence. Pour into a 23cm (9 inch) deep sided greased and lined sponge tin. Sprinkle top of sponge with more caster sugar to give a crisp surface. Bake in preheated oven 180C, 350F, Gas Mark 4 for 30 minutes. When cool, split the sponge, fill with fresh homemade strawberry jam and whipped cream.

BLACKCURRANT JAM

This is a good jam for beginners, as it sets so easily, make sure you add the sugar warmed and not too soon, otherwise the blackcurrants will harden.

Yields 2¼ kg (5lb)

Ingredients:
900g (2lb) blackcurrants
850ml (1½ pints) water
1.35kg (3lb) sugar

Remove currants from the stalks. If the fruit is dirty, wash and drain thoroughly. Put the fruit into a preserving pan with the water, and simmer gently to soften fruit. As the pulp thickens, stir frequently to prevent burning. Add the sugar, stir over a low heat until dissolved, then boil rapidly until setting point is reached. Test for setting, when set, skim and pot into warm jars and cover.

GOOSEBERRY JAM

It's best to pick or buy gooseberries when they are green before they have ripened or turned colour, it's one of my favourite jams and is delicious on scones with clotted cream!

Yields 2¼ kg (5lb)

Ingredients:
1kg (2¼lb) gooseberries, topped, tailed & washed
600ml (1 pint) water
1.35kg (3lb) sugar

Put the fruit into a preserving pan or large saucepan with the water. Simmer gently until the fruit is soft. Then add the sugar and stir over a very low heat until dissolved. Bring to the boil and boil rapidly until setting point is reached. Skim, and pot into warmed jars and cover.

REDCURRANT LIQUEUR

This easy to make fruit flavoured liqueur is made with redcurrants, but can be made equally as well with loganberries or blackcurrants. Serve it in small liqueur glasses, or make into a long drink with lemonade and ice. Delicious on a hot summer's day. It's also ideal to drink at Christmas time, if you can keep it that long!

Ingredients:
600ml (1 pint) white rum or vodka
450g (1lb) redcurrants
350g (12oz) sugar (granulated or caster)
3 blanched almonds

Pour the rum or vodka into a wide-necked jar and add the lightly crushed redcurrants and almonds. Cover and stand in a cool, dark place for a month, stirring every day. Drain off the liquid, pressing out all the juice. Add the sugar and stir until dissolved. Pour into small bottles and cork well. Keep for at least 6 months before using.

Contents – August

August

*W*ith all the soft fruits still with us, August is the month when I make pies and puddings to put away in my freezer ready to bring out during the winter months when summer is just a memory. And this month brings us the welcome arrival of plums, greengages and English apples, all just waiting to be made and baked into juicy pies and buttery crumbles. Variations on summer pies are endless and delicious, and whether sweet or savoury they can be served hot or cold, and made well in advance and re-heated.

So in this chapter I have included a special Crab Quiche and an Apple and Cider Pie, as well as other favourites of mine for this month. We still have plenty of salads with us too, from the Cos lettuce and little Gem, to Radicchio and Rocket, all adding colour and freshness to brighten up those quick summer salad meals and barbecues. Tomatoes and cucumbers are cheap too this month, especially on market stalls, so it's a good time to make sweet pickles and preserves.

CHILLED TOMATO SOUP

A delicious and colourful soup to serve as a first course at a dinner party, with the green chives complementing its rich orange colour.

Serves 6.

Ingredients:

900g (2lb) tomatoes, skinned
Sugar to taste
300ml (½ pint) milk

1 small onion
300ml (½ pint) single cream
Salt and pepper

Liquidize skinned tomatoes. Stir in cream and milk and chill in fridge. About half an hour before serving stir in 1 teaspoonful of grated onion, salt, pepper and sugar to taste. Serve with diced cucumber and a few chopped chives.

SMOKED TROUT MOUSSE

This is one of my favourite starters, but more often than not it's eaten for lunch in our household, especially in summer time, when all it needs is some triangles of hot brown toast and butter, and a green salad to accompany it.

Serves 4-6.

Ingredients:

350g (12oz) smoked trout
Salt & black pepper
Juice of ½ lemon

110g (4oz) cottage cheese
150g (5oz) soured cream

Remove skin and bones from fish and flake into liquidizer. Sieve cottage cheese and add with soured cream to the fish. Blend until smooth. Season to taste with salt, pepper and lemon juice. Spoon into individual ramekin dishes and chill in fridge. Sprinkle chopped parsley around edges and serve with fingers of buttered toast. Freezes well.

WALDORF SALAD

When I've plenty of eating apples left in the fruit bowl I make this salad. It's low in calories too, providing you go easy on the mayonnaise!

Serves 4.

Ingredients:
450g (1lb) red eating apples, cored
300ml (½ pint) mayonnaise
1 teaspoon caster sugar
1 lettuce separated into leaves
2 tablespoons lemon juice
50g (2oz) shelled walnuts, chopped
2-3 sticks of celery chopped

Slice apples (leaving the peel on) fairly thin and dice. Dip apples in a dressing made of lemon juice, sugar and two tablespoons of mayonnaise. Top with the remaining mayonnaise and set aside for 30 minutes. Add celery and walnuts and mix thoroughly. Serve piled into a glass dish lined with lettuce leaves.

LOW FAT CORONATION CHICKEN

A popular dish to serve in summer, it can be made well in advance leaving it in the fridge until it is needed.

Serves 4.

Ingredients:
450g (1lb) lean cooked chicken
16 cherry tomatoes
4 tsp mild curry paste
As much lettuce as you like!
Freshly ground black pepper
2 tablespoons of mango chutney
3 sticks celery
1 medium peach or nectarine, stoned
2 tablespoons 0% fromage frais
35g (1½oz) cashew nuts
Few sprigs of parsley to garnish

Chop chicken into bite-sized pieces, and chop celery. Halve tomatoes and cut peach into bite sized pieces. Mix curry paste, chutney and fromage frais together, blending well. Coat chicken and peach with mixture. Line a serving dish with lettuce and add the coated chicken and fruit with tomatoes, celery and nuts. Season with pepper and chill well before serving, garnish with a few sprigs of parsley.

GLAZED PORK CHOPS

This is a very easy recipe and a tasty way to serve pork. If there is sufficient space when you are grilling the chops, you can add some peeled and cored apple rings, sprinkled with brown sugar and dotted with butter, and grilled on pieces of foil beside the chops.

Serves 4.

Ingredients:

4 lean loin pork chops
4 heaped teaspoons soft brown sugar
4 level teaspoons of ready
   made mustard

A little chopped sage
Salt & pepper

Sprinkle the chops on both sides with salt and pepper. Mix the sugar and mustard together and spread it evenly over the chops on each side. Allow the grill at least 3 minutes to reach its full heat, and then place the chops under it on the grill rack. Give the chops 2 minutes on each side at full heat, then reduce the heat and cook the chops for approximately 6 minutes on each side, sprinkling a little chopped sage on top of each chop for the last 3 minutes of cooking.

MEAT LOAF

This loaf is quite generous in proportion, and I find there is usually some left over to cut out cold and serve with a salad.

Serves 6.

Ingredients:

50g (2oz) mushrooms,
   cleaned & chopped
3 large garlic cloves, crushed
1 teaspoon chopped thyme
450g (1lb) minced beef
4 slices of white bread with
   crusts removed
2 large eggs, beaten
1 tablespoon garlic mayonnaise
¼ teaspoon cayenne pepper

50g (2oz) butter
1 medium onion, peeled & chopped
2 tablespoons chopped rosemary
2 teaspoons chopped sage
450g (1lb) minced pork
50g (2oz) smoked back bacon,
   derinded & finely chopped
225ml (8fl oz) chicken cube stock
1½ teaspoon ready-made mustard

Melt half the fat in frying pan and cook mushrooms for 5 minutes, add garlic and 2 tablespoons of chicken stock and cook for a further 3 minutes. Stir in herbs. Soak the bread in the remaining stock, then squeeze dry and tear bread into pieces. Add bread to the meat with the beaten eggs, mix thoroughly and season with 1 tablespoon salt and 1 teaspoon black pepper. Put into a 25.5 x 15cm (10 x 6 inch) baking tin. Mix mayonnaise, mustard and cayenne pepper and brush over the top of meat loaf. Bake in preheated oven 180C, 350F, Gas Mark 4 for 1-1½ hours until loaf is cooked through and nicely browned.

LAMB FILLET WITH NOODLES

This recipe takes a little while to prepare, but if you've the time, it's well worth the effort.

Serves 4-6.

Ingredients:

1 lamb fillet
50g (2oz) pine nuts
½ lemon
150ml (5fl oz) red wine
2-3 tablespoons grated nutmeg
A little butter and seasoning

1 bunch of spring onions
1 teaspoon chopped rosemary
1 packet noodles (enough for 4-6)
300ml (½ pint) beef stock cube
300ml (½ pint) olive oil

Marinade lamb in lemon juice, oil, rosemary and salt and pepper. Cut onions into rounds. Heat oil in large pan and fry lamb over a high heat. Keep the meat warm while you fry the onions. Then fry the pine nuts, set aside with the lamb and keep warm. Deglaze the pan with red wine. Cook the noodles in boiling water, drain and toss in butter with salt and pepper and freshly grated nutmeg. Add the stock to the wine and bring to the boil. Bring the sauce to a simmer, thickening if necessary. Slice lamb, put onions and pine nuts on the top and noodles around the edge of the meat, pour sauce over the meat and serve with a fresh vegetable.

CRAB QUICHE

Nowadays we make quiches containing fillings of almost anything we have in our store cupboard, even leftovers, but this quiche is a special summer occasion one, and using crab as a filling makes it a bit different. A crisp 1997 Penedes Blanc Seleccio wine with its delicate and subtle lemon nuances, goes well with the crabmeat.

Serves 6.

Ingredients:

175g (6oz) shortcrust pastry
225ml (8fl oz) double cream
225g (8oz) crabmeat
  (fresh, frozen or tinned)
Salt & black pepper, & Cayenne pepper

2 eggs, plus 1 egg yolk
1 tablespoon dry sherry
2 rounded tablespoons grated
  Parmesan cheese

Grease a 20.5cm (8 inch) flan tin. Roll out the shortcrust pastry to 5mm (¼ inch) thick on lightly floured surface and use to line flan tin. Remove meat from fresh crab and use equal quantities of brown and white meat. Alternatively, thaw or drain the prepared crab meat. Flake the meat into a bowl, and beat together the eggs and egg yolk, cream and sherry in a mixing bowl. Blend in the crabmeat. Add cheese and season to taste with salt and freshly ground black pepper and cayenne. Spoon the mixture into the flan case and bake in centre of preheated oven 190C, 375F, Gas Mark 5 for 40 minutes, until the quiche is golden and set. Serve hot or cold as a first course, or with a tossed green salad as a main course.

MIXED BERRY FOOL

This is a very low-fat fruity berry dessert, but if you want to spoil yourself a little, then top it with a scoop of your favourite ice cream.

Serves 4.

Ingredients:

450g (1lb) rhubarb, trimmed
175g (6oz) fresh raspberries
225g (8oz) fresh strawberries,
  cleaned & hulled
3x150g (5oz) cartons of low fat yoghurt

400g (14oz) 0% fromage frais
75g (3oz) fresh redcurrants
75g (3oz) fructose *(or any low
  calorie sweetener)*

Cut rhubarb into bite-sized pieces and place in a non-stick pan. Cover and simmer gently for 5-6 minutes until tender. Remove from heat, cool and stir in fructose or sweetener. Divide rhubarb purée between four sundae glasses. Mix together the yoghurt and fromage frais, and divide between the glasses. Top with a selection of the fruits, and chill well before serving.

GREENGAGE CRUMBLE

The small round golden-yellow greengages make their brief appearance this month, and I try to make the most of this fruit while it's here in puddings and tarts, and the odd pot of jam too!

Serves 6.

Ingredients:
450g (1lb) ripe greengages	175g (6oz) caster sugar
75g (3oz) butter	175g (6oz) plain flour

Halve the greengages and remove the stones. Place the greengages in an ovenproof dish and sprinkle with one third of the sugar. Bake in preheated oven 190C, 375C, Gas Mark 5 for 10 minutes. Rub butter into flour and stir in the remaining sugar. Sprinkle over the cooked fruit to cover completely. Return to oven and cook for a further 40 minutes. Serve warm with custard or cream. Or you can make this apricot purée, which goes well with the greengages. Apricot purée: Cover 225g (8oz) fresh apricots or 110g (4oz) dried apricots in cold water and poach uncovered until tender. Drain, and rub through a sieve. Flavour purée with sugar and lemon rind to give it a sharp taste.

BAKED PEARS

For this dish you need pears that are almost ripe, it doesn't need much preparation and can be quickly assembled and cooked in no time at all.

Serves 4.

Ingredients:
2 dessert pears, almost ripe	150ml (¼ pint) double cream
50g (2oz) demerara sugar	4 ramekin dishes

Peel and quarter the pears and cut out the cores. Cut the fruit into bite-sized chunks and put them into the ramekin dishes. Mix the cream with all but a sprinkling of the demerara sugar and pour it over the pears. Bake in preheated oven 180C, 350F, Gas Mark 4 for 20-25 minutes. Sprinkle with remaining demerara sugar before serving.

APPLE AND CIDER PIE

This month sees the arrival of English apples, with Discovery one of the first to arrive, and my recipes for apples are endless, but I've included this particular one, as it's a firm family favourite. It's a good idea to make several of these pies in August to put in your freezer ready for when the English fruit season starts to get scarce.

Serves 6.

Ingredients:
275g (10oz) plain flour
25g (1oz) caster sugar
1 large egg yolk
2-3 tablespoons water
150g (5oz) unsalted butter,
   chilled & diced

Filling:
75g (3oz) unsalted butter
110g (4oz) caster sugar
50g (2oz) raisins
600ml (1 pint) medium-dry cider
Grated zest of l lemon
Milk for glazing
8 Granny Smith apples, peeled,
   cored & thickly sliced

Place flour and butter into a mixing bowl, mix with tips of fingers (or whiz in a food processor) until mixture resembles fine breadcrumbs. Add sugar, egg yolk and sufficient water to bind together into a ball. Wrap in cling film and chill in fridge for about an hour.

To make filling: Melt butter in large frying pan or saucepan. Gently sauté apples for 12 minutes until translucent. Sprinkle over caster sugar and cook for a further 2 minutes. Pour over the cider and simmer for another 2-3 minutes, then remove apples, add raisins and lemon zest, set aside in a bowl. Cook remaining syrup until it is reduced and thick. Sprinkle some flour on work surface and roll out two thirds of pastry and line a 20.5cm (8 inch) flan tin. Trim edges of pastry and paint the rim with milk. Pile fruit into case and pour over syrup. Roll out remaining pastry and lay on top of fruit. With the tip of a knife crimp edges of pastry to seal, trim edges and use leftover pastry to decorate with leaves. Glaze pastry with milk and sprinkle with caster sugar. Bake in preheated oven 190C, 375F, Gas Mark 5 for 35-40 minutes until crisp and golden brown. Serve hot with a jug of homemade custard or cream.

GOOSEBERRY FLAN

This flan is best made well in advance and served cold, it's a delicious way of eating gooseberries and you can use apples or cherries in the same recipe.

Serves 6.

Ingredients:
225g (8oz) plain flour
Pinch of salt
110g (4oz) butter
25g (1oz) caster sugar
1 small egg yolk

Filling:
2 small egg yolks
35g (1½oz) vanilla sugar
150ml (¼ pint) double cream
75ml (3fl oz pint) milk
225g (8oz) gooseberries, topped & tailed

Make pastry in the usual way and line 20.5cm (8 inch) flan tin. Whisk egg yolks with sugar and then add cream and milk. Fill flan case with gooseberries and pour over custard mixture. Bake in preheated oven 220C, 425F, Gas Mark 7 for 25 minutes. Sprinkle the surface of the flan with a little caster sugar and return to the oven for another 5 minutes. Serve cold.

LEMON, DATE AND NUT FINGERS

This recipe was given to me by Win Gage who runs a local craft shop and tearoom in the Suffolk village of Monks Eleigh, where these biscuits are very popular with customers.

Makes about 10 biscuits.

Ingredients:
225g (8oz) sweet biscuits, crushed
110g (4oz) chopped dates
1 small can of condensed milk

Rind & juice of 1 lemon
110g (4oz) chopped nuts
Sieved icing sugar

Mix together biscuits, lemon rind, juice, chopped dates and nuts, add milk to bind. Coat an 18cm (7 inch) square tin (or a small Swiss roll tin) with icing sugar. Spoon mixture into tin and bake in preheated oven 190C, 375F, Gas Mark 5 for 25 minutes until golden brown. Cool in tin and sprinkle with icing sugar, then cut into fingers or squares.

COFFEE CREAM BISCUITS

These biscuits are real teatime treats, and if you're not too keen on the coffee flavour then try butter icing flavoured with vanilla or chocolate.

Makes about 8-10 biscuits.

Ingredients:

175g (6oz) self-raising flour
50g (2oz) golden granulated sugar
1 teaspoon instant coffee, dissolved
  with 1 teaspoon of hot water

75g (3oz) butter
1 egg yolk

Rub butter into flour with fingertips, add sugar and mix to a stiff paste with separated egg yolk and coffee. Alternatively, a food processor will do the job quicker. The mixture will be quite dry at this stage, but just press it together in your hands to form about 16-20 small balls the size of a walnut. Place on a greased baking sheet and cook in preheated oven 200C, 400F, Gas Mark 6 for about 10 minutes, until firm and golden brown. Cool on a wire tray and sandwich biscuits together in twos with coffee cream made by mixing together 110g (4oz) icing sugar, 50g (2oz) butter and 1 teaspoon of instant coffee blended with 1 teaspoon of hot water. Dredge with icing sugar and store in an airtight tin.

SMALL HONEY CAKES

These little cakes or buns are a good cake tin standby, and go well with a cup of coffee for 'elevenses'.

Makes 12-18.

Ingredients:

75g (3oz) butter
2 eggs
1 tablespoon hot water
50g (2oz) honey

½ teaspoon vanilla essence
110g (4oz) self-raising flour
25g (1oz) caster sugar

Cream together the butter, sugar and honey until light and fluffy. Add the vanilla essence, beat in the eggs one at a time, fold in the sieved flour and hot water, and mix well. Fill greased bun tins two thirds full and bake in preheated oven 200C, 400F, Gas Mark 6 for 15 minutes. Turn out and cool on cake rack, ice with lemon glacé icing.

BANANA TEA BREAD

This recipe came via a friend in Canada, but is very much like the English version of tea bread. It will freeze and keep very well for at least three months.

Ingredients:

200g (7oz) self-raising flour
½ teaspoon of salt
160g (5½oz) caster sugar
450g (1lb) mashed bananas

¼ teaspoon bicarbonate of soda
60g (2½oz) butter
2 eggs, beaten

Sift together flour, baking soda and salt. Cream butter and sugar. Add eggs and beat well. Peel and mash bananas, and beat into egg mixture. Mix in flour, taking care not to over beat. Pour into a greased and lined loaf tin 20.5cm x 11.5cm x 9cm (8½ x 4½ x 3 inches). Bake in a preheated oven 180C, 350F, Gas Mark 4 for about an hour until the tea bread is cooked through.

BLACKCURRANT & ALMOND SLICES

If you've just made blackcurrant jam and have some left over, then use it to make these strudel slices, it's a good way of finishing up what's left at the bottom of your preserving pan, but you can use almost any type of jam in this recipe.

Makes 12.

Ingredients:

225g (8oz) plain flour
110g (4oz) butter
110g (4oz) caster sugar plus 2
   tablespoons caster sugar
Icing sugar for dusting

110g (4oz) semolina
50g (2oz) chopped almonds
225g (8oz) blackberry jam
   (preferably homemade)

Put the flour, semolina and 110g (4oz) of caster sugar into a large mixing bowl and mix well. Rub in the butter until the mixture just starts to stick together. Spoon half the mixture into a greased 18cm x 28cm (7 x 11 inch) non-stick baking tin. Use the back of a spoon to press the mixture into an even solid base, and then spread the blackcurrant jam evenly over it. Mix the chopped almonds and the 2 tablespoons of caster sugar with the other half of the mixture to make a crumble. Sprinkle it over the blackcurrant jam. Bake in preheated oven 170C, 325F, Gas Mark 3 for 35 minutes until golden. Allow to cool in the tin for about 15 minutes, and then cut into 12 bars and leave to cool for another 5 minutes. Place the bars on a cooling rack, and when completely cooled dust with icing sugar.

RUNNER BEAN CHUTNEY

I'm asked for this recipe time and time again by friends. It's an excellent chutney and keeps really well.

Ingredients:

900g (2lb) runner beans
(when trimmed & sliced)
1 heaped tablespoon cornflour
1 heaped tablespoon dry mustard
450g (1lb) brown sugar

1 tablespoon turmeric
450g (1lb) demerara sugar
850ml (1½ pints) vinegar
700g (1½lb) onions (when
peeled & chopped)
1 dessertspoon salt water

Prepare the vegetables. Cook sliced beans in well-salted water until tender. Cook chopped onions in 300ml (½ pint) vinegar. Mix dry ingredients to smooth paste with vinegar. Strain cooked beans, add remaining vinegar and cook for 10 minutes, add sugar and the rest of the ingredients and boil for a further 15 minutes. Bottle and cover.

TOMATO CHUTNEY

This is another popular chutney, and I usually make several pounds this month when there are plenty of tomatoes about. I use half dessert apples and half cooking apples in this recipe so that it's not too sharp tasting.

Makes about 3.2kg (7lb)

Ingredients:

700g (1½lb) red tomatoes *(skinned)*
850ml (1½ pints) best malt vinegar
10g (½oz) mustard seed
25g (1oz) cooking salt

450g (1lb) dates
450g (1lb) onions
350g (12oz) sugar
450g (1lb) apples, half dessert
& half cooking *(when peeled)*

Peel and core apples, and chop finely together with dates and onions. Skin tomatoes and add to ingredients. Boil for 1½ hours. Leave to cool, then store in jars.

PLUM JAM

Pick ripe juicy dessert plums for jam making, and be sure to pick out the stones before you pot it up.

Yields approximately 2¼ kg (5 lb)

Ingredients:
1.35kg (3lb) plums
1.35kg (3lb) granulated sugar
150ml (¼ pint) water

Remove stalks and put the washed plums into a preserving pan with the water (add extra water if you are using cooking plums). Poach slowly until the fruit is well broken down. Add the sugar and stir over a low heat until dissolved, then boil rapidly, removing the stones as they rise to the surface. Keep testing for setting point by putting a teaspoon of the jam on to a saucer and letting it get cold, I usually put mine in the fridge to save time. After boiling for about 10 minutes the jam should have reached setting point, you can then skim, pot and cover.

GREENGAGE JAM

If you want to make greengage jam, use the same quantity of ingredients and proceed as for the plum jam above. I always look out for the new season's greengages on fruit market stalls; if you wander round just before the stallholders are packing-up to leave, you can usually buy a box of greengages cheap – they may be a bit over-ripe, but they will make excellent jam.

Contents – September

September

September is the month when summer fades into autumn and there is a definite chill in the air. The nights begin to draw in, although we do get days that are bright and sunny giving us a reminder of summer. It's the last month we can reasonably expect to eat out of doors, and it's a busy time in the kitchen for making jams, jellies, pickles and chutneys to store away for the winter months.

So in this chapter there will be recipes making the most of the season's crops, using blackberries, plums, and the fruit vegetables that abound in September including courgettes, marrows, aubergines and peppers. There are lots of varieties of homegrown apples and pears, and plums and damsons, which will make those delicious autumn puddings, including many old favourites. Harvest time will be here and celebrated in beautifully decorated churches up and down the country, and it's a month I like to enjoy and savour before the winter really sets in.

CREAM OF CAULIFLOWER SOUP

There's always plenty of cauliflowers about at this time of the year and making this soup is a good way of using them up. Although they can taste rather bland, putting a teaspoon of curry powder in the soup does help to give more flavour.

Serves 4-6.

Ingredients:

1 fairly large cauliflower,
  broken into florets
10g (½oz) flour
300ml (½ pint) water
1 chicken stock cube

2 medium onions, peeled & chopped
1 teaspoon curry powder
300ml (½ pint) milk
25g (1oz) butter
Seasoning

Cook the cauliflower in boiling, salted water. Break it up and reserve some of the liquid to make up the 300ml (½ pint water). Melt butter in saucepan and add the onion, cover with lid and let the onion soften. Add the curry powder and cook for a further few minutes. Dissolve the stock cube in some of the hot liquid from the cauliflower and add this, and all the rest of the ingredients, to the saucepan. Stir well. Put into liquidiser and when blended return to saucepan. Bring to the boil to thicken. Adjust seasoning and consistency to taste.

CELERIAC SOUP

This vegetable makes a thick nourishing soup with a delicious root flavour coming through it, but it will not freeze because of the added egg yolks and cream.

Serves 4-6.

Ingredients:

3 roots celeriac
60g (2½oz) butter
2 blades mace
Salt and pepper
2 egg yolks
Croutons to serve

1 medium onion, peeled & chopped
850ml (1½ pints) milk
1 bay leaf
35g (1½ oz) flour
2 tablespoons cream

Slice and lightly fry celeriac with onion in butter until soft. Pass through a sieve or liquidise. Bring the milk to the boil with herbs and seasoning. Simmer for 15 minutes. Blend flour with sieved vegetables and butter, add milk. Cook over low heat until thickened. Blend egg yolks and cream with a little of the soup, stir into remaining soup. Reheat gently and serve with croutons.

SALMON MOUSSE

A lovely creamy mousse, ideal to serve as a starter or you can serve it as a light lunch with a crisp green salad and brown bread and butter.

Serves 4.

Ingredients:

225g (8oz) cooked salmon
225g (8oz) cream cheese
2 tablespoons mayonnaise
25g (1oz) fresh white breadcrumbs
Salt and pepper to taste

110g (4oz) smoked salmon
Juice half a lemon
Pinch of paprika
2 tablespoons whipped cream

Blend salmon in a food processor to a purée. Add all the other ingredients and blend together. Turn into a mould and leave in the fridge until set. Unmould and serve when needed.

SARDINE AND SPINACH PATÉ

This is an unusual paté and it freezes quite well, and I find spinach is easier to prepare if washed in warm water.

Serves 4-6.

Ingredients:

450g (1lb) leaf spinach
110g (4oz) butter, softened
1 teaspoon pale French mustard
Freshly ground black pepper

1 tin sardines
Juice of half a lemon
Salt

Wash the spinach and pull out the thick stalks. Put the still wet leaves in a saucepan without water. Cover closely with the lid and cook over moderate heat for 4-5 minutes, giving the pan an occasional shake and toss. Drain and press the spinach, then chop or liquidize it very finely. When cold, beat in the sardines and butter together to a soft paste. Flavour with mustard, salt, if needed, pepper and lemon juice. Chill well before serving with hot toast.

TROUT IN TOMATO SAUCE WITH NOODLES

This dish is quick and easy to prepare, and can be on the table ready to serve in 20 minutes – true!

Serves 4.

Ingredients:

350g (12oz) flat noodles
1 large onion peeled & chopped
225g (8oz) mushrooms, sliced
1 tablespoon tomato purée
Salt and black pepper
50g (2oz) polyunsaturated margarine

3 tablespoons olive oil
1 large garlic clove, finely chopped
4 trout fillets, skinned & roughly diced
300ml (½ pint) low fat cream fraiche
2 tablespoons fresh basil, chopped

Bring some water to the boil in a large saucepan. Add the noodles and boil for 10-12 minutes. When just soft, drain and mix in 1 tablespoon of the olive oil and place on a warm serving dish. Meanwhile, in a large deep frying pan, melt the margarine with the remaining olive oil. Add the onion and garlic and fry until the onion is just tender. Add the mushrooms and cook until soft. Stir in the trout, tomato purée and crème fraiche, and simmer for 5 minutes. Season with salt and pepper and stir in basil. Pour sauce over noodles and serve with crusty bread and a side salad.

STUFFED FIELD MUSHROOMS

September is such a good month in which to gather some of the largest and finest tasting mushrooms. These stuffed mushrooms can be served as a main course with sautéed potatoes, tomatoes and courgettes, or as a substantial starter.

Serves 1 per person as a starter, or 2 per person as a main course.

Ingredients:

8 large firm field mushrooms
6 streaky rashers of bacon,
   cut into strips
2 tablespoons flour
Salt and pepper to taste
1 tablespoon chopped parsley

50g (2oz) butter
1 large onion, peeled & chopped
2 teaspoons chopped sage (fresh if
   possible)
225ml (8fl oz) milk
Parsley to garnish

Clean mushrooms, break off stalks, chop them and set aside. Arrange mushroom caps on a greased baking sheet. Heat the butter in a large frying pan and fry the bacon, then set aside on a warm plate. Add the onion, bacon, sage and mushroom stalks to the juices in pan, cover and soften. Stir in the flour until absorbed, then remove the pan from the heat and stir in the milk, a little at a time, until absorbed. Return to the heat and simmer to thicken. Add the bacon and parsley and season to taste. Spoon filling into the mushroom caps and bake in preheated oven 180C, 350F, Gas Mark 4 for about 30 minutes. Garnish with parsley and serve.

STUFFED SHOULDER OF LAMB WITH VEGETABLES

One pot or dish meals need very little attention once they are prepared and assembled, and this recipe is a complete course in which the meat, vegetables, potatoes and gravy are all cooked together. Once it's in the oven you can forget all about it, until it's cooked and ready to serve.

Serves 6.

Ingredients:

2kg (4½lb) shoulder of lamb
225g (8oz) button mushrooms
50g (2oz) dripping
300ml (½ pint) cider
1 level dessertspoon tomato purée
450g (1lb) carrots, peeled &
    cut into quarters
900g (2lb) potatoes, peeled &
    cut into halves

A sprig of rosemary
450g (1lb) onions, peeled & sliced
3 level tablespoons plain flour
150ml (¼ pint) lamb stock cube
Salt & black pepper
2 sticks celery, scrubbed & cut
    into 2.5cm (1 inch) lengths
1 medium parsnip, peeled & cut into
    2.5cm (1 inch) rings

Wipe shoulder of lamb with a damp cloth. Then using a sharp knife, loosen the meat all the way round the flat blade bone right down to the joint on both sides; this makes it easy to remove before carving. Melt the dripping in a large roasting tin on top of the cooker and brown the meat as evenly as possible over a fairly strong heat. Remove the meat and set aside to keep warm. Fry the prepared vegetables in batches, adding enough to cover the base of the roasting tin, and turning them occasionally to brown them lightly all over. Stir the flour into the last batch of vegetables and stir on the heat for a minute or two. Add the cider and stock with the tomato purée and stir over a gentle heat until the gravy is smooth and comes to the boil; the liquid from the vegetables will thin the gravy. Stir in the rest of the vegetables and season with salt and black pepper, bring all to the boil. Sprinkle the meat with salt, lay it on top of the vegetables and add the sprig of

111

rosemary. Cover the meat and vegetables with a large piece of kitchen foil, tucking it carefully under the rim of the roasting tin. Put joint into a preheated oven 180C, 350F, Gas Mark 4 for 2 hours, or until the meat is cooked right through. Transfer the lamb onto a hot dish and surround it with the vegetables, and serve the rest of vegetables and gravy separately.

SPICY PORK MINCE

This is an economical dish, but tastes really delicious, and all the ingredients can be cooked in the same utensil. It doesn't take long to cook and heats up well too.

Serves 4.

Ingredients:

450g (1lb) lean pork mince
2 cloves garlic, crushed
Salt and black pepper
175g (6oz) long grain, easy cook rice
225g (8oz) potato, scrubbed,
   but with skin left on
2 tablespoons fresh coriander,
   chopped (optional)

1 large onion, peeled & chopped
850ml (1½ pints) pork stock cube
150g (5oz) frozen peas
2 tablespoons medium curry paste
110g (4oz) mushrooms, wiped &
   quartered

In a large non-stick wok or saucepan, dry fry the mince for about 4-5 minutes. Add the onion and garlic and cook for a further 2-3 minutes. Then add the stock, rice, potato, curry paste and seasoning. Bring to the boil and simmer for 15 minutes. Add the remaining ingredients and simmer for approximately 5 minutes until the rice is cooked and the water is absorbed. Serve with poppadoms or crusty bread.

BEEF PARCELS

I often make these beef parcels in batches and freeze them ready for use when required. Served on a dish surrounded by cooked fluffy rice they make a tasty meal.

Serves 4.

Ingredients:

450g (1lb) top side beef	1 large onion, peeled & chopped
110g (4oz) chopped cooked ham	2 carrots, peeled & finely chopped
1 teaspoon mixed herbs	2 tablespoons Worcester sauce
2 teaspoons flour	2 tablespoons tomato purée
150ml (¼ pint) beef stock	Parsley
(stock cube will do)	

Cut beef into 4 thick slices and batten out. Mix all the other prepared ingredients together including sauce, flour and seasoning and spread evenly on the beef slices. Roll into equal sized parcels and place in a casserole dish, then pour over the stock. Cook in a preheated oven 180C, 350F, Gas Mark 4 for about 45 minutes. You can cook this dish in a combination microwave oven set at 250C for 20-25 minutes. Garnish with parsley before serving.

POTATO SCONES

These scones are good eaten just as they are, or with almost anything, but I think they are best with bacon and eggs.

Makes about 10-12 scones.

Ingredients:

225g (8oz) cooked potatoes	50g (2oz) plain flour
Half a level teaspoon salt	A knob of lard or butter
1 tablespoon finely chopped parsley	

Mash potatoes very smoothly, using an electric mixer. Put flour, salt, chopped parsley and potatoes on a floured surface, and work the flour into the potatoes. Sprinkle surface with more flour and roll out mixture as thinly as possible. Cut into small rounds with a scone cutter, and heat a thick-based pan or griddle to a fairly hot heat, covering the bottom of the pan or griddle with a little oil or butter. Cook scones in two batches, pricking them all over with a fork. Cook for 2-3 minutes on each side or until golden brown and allow to cool slightly before serving.

BLACKCURRANT AND PEAR COBBLER

This month will see the last of the blackcurrants, and I try to make as many desserts as I can with this delicious little berry. I'm lucky enough to have a fruit farm near where I live in Suffolk, and I make sure I pick plenty of blackcurrants to make jams and puddings, and freeze some for the winter months. Pears with blackcurrants make an unusual, but surprising combination, and if you use fairly ripe ones they give an added sweet syrupy flavour to the pudding.

Serves 4-6.

Ingredients:
225g (8oz) plain flour
2 teaspoons baking powder
35g (1½oz) butter
50g (2oz) caster sugar
150ml (¼ pint) milk

For the filling:
3 fairly ripe pears, thinly peeled & sliced
450g (1lb) fresh blackcurrants
50g (2oz) granulated sugar
1 small beaten egg

Sift flour with baking powder and rub in the butter until the mixture resembles fine breadcrumbs. Stir in the sugar and then add the milk and mix to a soft dough. Knead on a lightly floured surface and set aside for 10-15 minutes. Mix the fruit with sugar and place in an ovenproof dish. Roll out the scone dough to 1cm (½ inch) thickness and cut into circles with a small pastry cutter and then arrange over the fruit. Glaze with the beaten egg and bake in a preheated oven 220C, 425F, Gas Mark 7 for 10 minutes, then reduce the heat to 180C, 350F, Gas Mark 4 and bake for a further 20 minutes. Serve with custard or whipped cream.

LEMON MOUSSE

This soufflé is a delicious light and tangy dessert, ideal to serve for a special dinner party, so I don't make it that often, but when I do, compliments abound!

Serves 6.

Ingredients:
3 eggs
10g (½oz) gelatine
Grated rind and juice of
  2 medium lemons
150ml (¼ pint) cream, partially whipped

175g (6oz) caster sugar
3-4 tablespoons water
A little extra cream & chopped
  nuts for decoration

Separate yolks and whites of the eggs. Beat the sugar into the yolks and then add lemon rind and juice. Whisk over a gentle heat until thick and a mousse-like consistency, remove and whisk for a further 2-3 minutes. Then dissolve gelatine in the water and add to the mixture. Whip up egg whites to firm peaks. Fold the cream into the mousse and then fold in the egg whites. Turn at once into a prepared deep soufflé dish and set aside in the fridge to chill. When ready to serve, pipe top with extra cream and sprinkle nuts around the edges.

BLACKBERRY AND APPLE CRUMBLE

You can make a crumble with almost any kind of fruit, but blackberries and apples are two of the most popular. This particular crumble has the added nuttiness of ground almonds and rolled oats, giving the dessert a crisp and crunchy topping with the juicy fruits underneath.

Serves 6.

Ingredients:
900g (2lb) Bramley apples, peeled,
    cored & chopped
350g (12oz) blackberries
    (preferably wild)
3 tablespoons caster sugar
Pinch of ground cinnamon

Topping:
50g (2oz) plain flour
50g (2oz) rolled oats
50g (2oz) butter diced
50g (2oz) ground almonds
50g (2oz) caster sugar

Place the apples and blackberries in a 1½ litre (2 pint) pie dish. Sprinkle the cinnamon and sugar over the fruit. Add 3 tablespoons water and set aside. Place the flour, ground almonds and oats in a mixing bowl. Add the butter and rub into the flour with fingertips until it resembles fine breadcrumbs. Add the sugar to the crumble and mix together, then spread the crumble over the fruit and bake in preheated oven 190C, 375F, Gas Mark 5 for at least 50 minutes, until the fruit is cooked and the top is crisp and golden. Serve hot with custard or single cream.

APPLE FRITTERS

I'm usually given more apples than I know what to do with at this time of the year, and when I run out of ideas what to do with them, I make a dish of apple fritters, piled high and sprinkled with sugar they make a perfect pudding or tidbit to fill a hungry corner.

Serves 4-6.

Ingredients:
225g (8oz) plain flour
425ml to 600ml (¾-1 pint) milk

2 eggs
Good pinch of salt

Put all the ingredients into a basin or large jug, and using an electric beater, beat up the batter until it forms bubbles. You should have enough batter for 4 apples. Peel and core 4 Bramley apples and slice into thin rings. Have some boiling hot fat in a frying pan, dip each ring in the batter and fry quickly until golden brown. Fry in batches, then drain on kitchen paper or greaseproof. Serve piping hot sprinkled liberally with caster sugar.
NB. You may have a quantity of batter left over, which you can use to make pancakes and then store them in your freezer.

115

BLACKCURRANT CAKE

This cake can double as a dessert served with cream, but is delicious eaten as a cake for tea dredged with icing sugar when cold.

Serves 6-8.

Ingredients:

110g (4oz) butter	175g (6oz) caster sugar
2 eggs	110g (4oz) self-raising flour
50g (2oz) ground rice	225g (8oz) blackcurrants

Cream the butter and sugar together until light and fluffy. Beat in the eggs one at a time in the flour and ground rice mixed together. Stir in the blackcurrants, making sure they are quite dry. Turn the mixture into a well-greased 20.5cm (8 inch) cake tin and bake in a preheated oven 180C, 350F, Gas Mark 4 for about 1 hour until well risen and brown.

BARA BRITH

This recipe originates from Wales, hence the name, and it disappears quickly whenever I make it, but it's delicious toasted if there is any left!

Ingredients:

350g (12oz) mixed dried fruit	300ml (½ pint) cold tea
1 egg	1 pinch mixed spice
350g (12oz) wholemeal flour	225g (8oz) demerara sugar

Using a medium sized mixing bowl soak the mixed fruit and sugar overnight in the cold tea. Sift the mixed spice and beaten egg into the flour and add to the mixed fruit and sugar. Mix well. Divide the mixture equally between 3 greased and lined 450g (1lb) loaf tins and bake for 1½-1¾ hours in preheated oven 170C, 325F, Gas Mark 3. Cool on cooling trays and serve sliced and buttered.

COCONUT CHERRY SLICES

These slices are a great favourite when I make them to sell at our village fetes and bazaars, and stored in an airtight tin they keep for at least 4 days.

Makes about 15.

Ingredients:
225g (8oz) self-raising flour
110g (4oz) butter
1 egg
Pinch of salt

For the topping:
150g (5oz) desiccated coconut
2 egg whites
110g (4oz) caster sugar
1 tablespoon plain flour
3 tablespoons raspberry jam
50g (2oz) glacé cherries, cut into quarters

Make pastry in the usual way and roll it out thinly to an oblong shape. Grease and line a Swiss roll tin, line it with the pastry and spread the jam over it. Now whisk up the egg whites until they are very stiff and add the coconut, cherries, sugar and flour. Spread this mixture evenly over the jam. Bake in preheated oven 190C, 375F, Gas Mark 5 for about 30 minutes, when the top should be golden brown. Cut into slices while hot, and remove from tin when cold.

GRANNY'S LIGHT FRUIT CAKE

This cake is one of the popular cut-and-come-again favourites, and over the years I've baked it so many times that I rarely have to look up the recipe.

Ingredients:
225g (8oz) self-raising flour
110g (4oz) caster sugar
110g (4oz) sultanas

110g (4oz) butter
2 eggs, well beaten
A little milk

Cream the butter and sugar until light and fluffy. Add the beaten eggs one at a time. Then gradually add the flour beating well. Mix in the sultanas and a little milk to make a soft consistency. Spoon into a greased and lined 450g (1lb) loaf tin and bake in preheated oven 180C, 350F, Gas Mark 4 for 45-60 minutes.

BLACKBERRY AND APPLE JELLY

This is the month for making jellies and jams, and I try not to let September pass without making this jelly, which is delicious spread on hot toast or just plain bread and butter.

Ingredients:
1.8kg (4lb) blackberries
1½ litres (2 pints) water

1.8kg (4lb) cooking apples
Granulated sugar

Rinse the fruit. Cut up the apples without peeling or coring. Simmer the blackberries and apples separately with the water for about 1 hour until the fruits are tender. Mash apples well and allow to drip through a jelly bag, and follow the same procedure for blackberries. Measure the juices and bring to the boil, then stir in the sugar 450g (1lb) to each 600ml (1 pint) of juice. Boil rapidly until it sets. Pot into warmed jars, cover with waxed discs and tie down.

PLUM AND APPLE CHUTNEY

Each year when the preserving season comes round I make this chutney, it keeps well, and has a sharp fruity taste, it goes well with cheese or cold pork, and makes tasty sandwiches.

Yields 2¼ kg (5lb)

Ingredients:
900g (2lb) cooking apples, peeled,
    cored & chopped
450g (1lb) plums, stoned & halved
1.35kg (3lb) onions, chopped
225g (8oz) seedless raisins
700g (1½lb) demerara sugar

225g (8oz) sultanas
600ml (1 pint) malt vinegar
1 tablespoon ground mixed spice
Grated rind & juice of 1 lemon
1 teaspoon salt

Place the apples and plums together in a stainless steel preserving pan with the remaining ingredients. Heat gently, stirring, until the sugar has dissolved, then simmer, uncovered, stirring occasionally, until the mixture is smooth and thick, with no excess liquid. Then pot and seal, and store for at least 6 weeks before using.

PICKLED PEACHES

These pickled peaches are delicious eaten with ham and cold meats at Christmas time, and September is the month when you'll find plenty of this fruit available on market stalls and in supermarkets, so make the most of the peach season.

Ingredients:

900g (2lb) ripe peaches

5cm (2 inch) cinnamon stick

225g (8 oz) soft light brown sugar

6 allspice berries

4 cloves

425ml (¾ pint) white wine vinegar

Pour boiling water over the peaches to loosen their skins. Peel and cut the fruit into quarters, removing the stones. Measure 150ml (¼ pint) water into a non-aluminium saucepan. Add the spices and sugar, simmer and stir until the sugar has dissolved. Add the vinegar and peaches and simmer for 4-5 minutes until the peaches begin to soften. Transfer the peaches to clean jars and pour over the cooking liquid, cover and store for 3 months before eating.

Contents – October

October

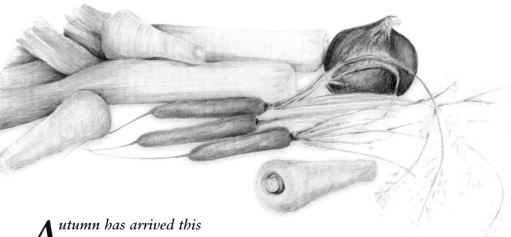

Autumn has arrived this month, with deep blue skies, brilliant sunshine, and in East Anglia where I live, we have the most gorgeous deep pink sunsets that never cease to amaze me. But on the down side we start to get the first of the frosts which means the last of our summer fruits and vegetables are doomed, but the new season's cabbages, leeks, parsnips and Swedes will all benefit from a nip of frost, and Brussels sprouts will be at their best once the frost has been on them. And, of course, the 1 October brings the beginning of the pheasant season – years ago when I lived in Somerset it was not unusual to find a brace or two on my doorstep, but nowadays supermarkets stock them, neatly dressed and packaged, and ready for the oven. It's also tidy up month, especially in the garden, and time to take stock in the kitchen as it gets nearer to December and Christmas!

HAM & PUMPKIN SOUP

There are plenty of pumpkins around during October, but if you're not too keen on them, try using squash or butternut which will work just as well; I think it's good to experiment with these lesser-known vegetables that have now crept into our supermarkets and shops.

Serves 4.

Ingredients:

1 kg (2¼lb) pumpkin, peeled,
   deseeded & cut into cubes
300g (10½oz) thick slices of ham cut
   into 2.5cm (1 inch) cubes
1 large onion, peeled &
   roughly chopped

50g (2oz) butter
1 tablespoon plain flour
Bunch of basil, roughly chopped
Salt & black pepper

Cook onion and half the pumpkin for 5 minutes until just starting to soften. Stir in the flour and mix well to absorb the butter. Add 600ml (1 pint) water, a little at a time, and stir until smooth. Bring to the boil and simmer for 25 minutes. Blend the soup until smooth, and add the remaining pumpkin, the ham and basil. Season to taste, return to heat and bring to the boil, simmer for 20 minutes, stirring occasionally until pumpkin is tender. Serve in 4 large soup bowls with warm crusty brown bread.

KEDGEREE

This is excellent served with courgettes, mushrooms, or ratatouille for a main meal, or on its own for a light lunch; I've even served it for breakfast!

Serves 3-4.

Ingredients:

450g (1lb) smoked haddock fillet,
   or cod fillet
110g (4oz) butter

3 hard-boiled eggs
175g (6oz) long grain rice

Cook the rice in boiling, salted water (or as directed). Cook fish removing all skin. Break into flakes, and chop the eggs. Melt some of the butter in a saucepan, but do not let it brown. Add fish, rice and eggs stirring well with a fork. Add more butter gradually with the saucepan over a low heat. The rice will absorb the butter and give the dish a heavy consistency. Season well with black pepper and serve hot.

MACKEREL BAKED IN CIDER

Mackerel is a favourite fish of mine, and I like to try out different ways of cooking it. I've found that baking it in cider gives the fish a more piquant flavour than when I've cooked it in white wine, and the mustard dressing gives the dish a finishing touch.

Serves 4.

Ingredients:
4 medium sized mackerel, filleted
25g (1oz) butter
1 large onion, peeled & sliced
2 dessert apples, peeled, cored & sliced
300ml (½ pint) dry cider
1 teaspoon chopped dill

Dressing:
2 teaspoons French mustard
1 teaspoon cider
1 tablespoon cornflour
150ml (5fl oz) low fat fromage frais
Salt & black pepper

Melt butter in ovenproof casserole and lightly fry the onion and apple until golden. Remove from the heat and add the cider, then the mackerel and dill. Cover with lid and bake in preheated oven 180C, 350F, Gas Mark 4 for 30 minutes. When cooked set aside on a warm dish. To make the dressing: Mix the cornflour with 2 tablespoons cold water and stir into the fromage frais. Stir the fromage frais into the cooking juices, bring to the boil and thicken. Add the mustard and cider, and season. Serve with mashed potatoes and broccoli.

PHEASANT IN WINE AND CREAM

This recipe is always popular with guests and easy to prepare, especially if you get oven ready birds, and if you are going to serve more than four people then you need to double up on the ingredients.

Serves 4.

Ingredients:
2 young plump pheasants
2 breakfast cups inexpensive red wine
2 fairly large cooking apples, peeled,
   cored & thinly sliced

600ml (1 pint) single cream
Salt & pepper

Season the birds and place in an ovenproof casserole. Pour over the wine, seal tightly with foil and cook in a preheated oven 180C, 350F, Gas Mark 4 for approximately 1½ hours until tender. Remove flesh from bird and set aside. Thicken the liquid in which the birds were cooked with a little cornflour, and gradually add the cream. Season to taste and add pheasant meat to the casserole, with thinly sliced apple, return to the oven and reheat for about 15-20 minutes. Serve with sauté potatoes and Brussels sprouts. The cooked birds and sauce can be frozen, omitting the cream.

LIVER AND ORANGE CASSEROLE

When the colder weather starts to set in I like to cook casseroles, and this dish makes a warm and nutritious meal. It can be reheated and goes well with buttered carrots, cabbage and mashed potatoes.

Serves 6.

Ingredients:

450g (1lb) lambs liver, thinly sliced
1 medium onion, peeled &
   finely chopped
425g (¾ pint) vegetable stock
   (stock cube will do)
Finely shredded rind of half an
   orange for garnish

35g (1½oz) dripping
4 level tablespoons flour
Grated rind & juice of 1 orange
Salt & pepper

Melt the dripping in an ovenproof casserole. Season the flour with pepper and salt, and toss the liver into it. Fry the liver briskly in the hot dripping, browning both sides. Remove liver and set aside. Add the chopped onion to the pan and cook gently until soft, then add the rest of the seasoned flour to absorb any fat. Blend in the stock, the orange juice and rind. Bring to the boil, stirring until thickened and season with salt and pepper. Cover and cook in preheated oven 170C, 325F, Gas Mark 3 for about half an hour. Sprinkle the top with the finely shredded orange rind and serve from casserole.

LOIN OF PORK WITH PINEAPPLE & DATE STUFFING

Loin of pork is one of the best buys for roasting, although it does have to have added flavours to offset its rather bland taste. Ask your butcher to bone the joint for you to make it easier for stuffing, and if you like crackling, then have this removed too and scored. To get a really crisp crackling put it into a separate dish from your joint, sprinkle it with salt and cook on the top shelf of your oven for about 30 minutes, finishing under the grill for a further 25 minutes.

Serves 4-6.

Ingredients:

1¼kg (2¾lb) lean loin of pork,
   boned & rolled

Glaze::

1 tablespoon lime marmalade blended
   with 1 tablespoon pineapple juice

For stuffing:
110g (4oz) fresh white breadcrumbs
1 small can of pineapple in natural juice
   (finely chopped & juice reserved)
25g (1oz) dates, chopped
1 lime, rind & juice (½ reserved for glaze)

Make stuffing by mixing breadcrumbs, pineapple, dates, lime rind and 4 tablespoons reserved lime and pineapple juice to bind.   At this stage you can either stuff the joint or shape stuffing into small balls. Cook joint in preheated oven 180C, 350F, Gas Mark 4 for about 1½-2 hours or until joint is cooked through and the juices run clear when tested with a skewer.
Serve with vegetable ribbons: 4 carrots, peeled and cut into ribbons, 2 courgettes, top and tailed, and cut into ribbons, 1 small celeriac, peeled and cut into ribbons. 1 tablespoon oil, 1 teaspoon honey, 1 teaspoon lemon juice, salt and black pepper. Toss the vegetables in the oil, honey and lemon juice in a flat roasting tin. Sprinkle with salt and pepper and roast for about 1 hour. Add roast potatoes to serve.

ROAST CHICKEN WITH ORANGE

This is one of the nicest ways to roast chicken. The orange and honey make the bird crisp and golden, and the flavour is delicious.

Serves 4.

Ingredients:

1.35kg (3lb) oven-ready chicken	2 oranges
50g (2oz) butter	2 tablespoons red wine
1 small glass red wine	1 dessertspoon honey
¼ teaspoon ginger	¼ teaspoon salt
1 teaspoon flour	

Put whole orange inside the chicken. Melt 50g (2oz) butter and pour over the breast and legs.   Place in a roasting tin and cook for 30 minutes in preheated oven 200C, 400F, Gas Mark 6 for 30 minutes. Meanwhile mix the honey, ginger, salt and the 2 tablespoons red wine in a cup. Take out chicken and brush all over with the mixture. Return to the oven with temperature lowered to 180C, 350F, Gas Mark 4 and cook for one hour, basting every 15 minutes. When chicken is cooked, remove from pan and set aside to keep warm, and make a sauce with juices in the pan, adding juice of the other orange, 1 teaspoon flour and 1 small glass of red wine. Bring to the boil and serve separately. Garnish chicken with grated rind of orange.

CHEESE AND ONION PIE

This is a good standby for the colder days, and can be eaten hot for a main course with a jacket potato, or cut out cold for a packed lunch.

Serves 6.

Ingredients:
350g (12oz) shortcrust pastry
  (ready made will do)

Filling:
225g (8oz) finely grated Cheddar cheese
450g (1lb) onions, peeled & chopped
25g (1oz) butter
50ml (2fl oz) milk
2 eggs
Salt & pepper

To prepare filling: Melt butter in a small saucepan. Add peeled and coarsely chopped onions and cook gently until lightly browned. Beat egg and milk together until well blended, and then stir in drained, cooked onion and finely grated cheese. Season well with salt and pepper to taste.

Roll out two thirds of the pastry into a round to fit the base and sides of a deep 23cm (9 inch) pie plate. Ease the pastry into the dish and trim off excess pastry. Damp pastry rim with water and turn filling into the centre. Roll out remaining pastry and trimmings into just over a 23cm (9 inch) round for the cover. Lift on to pie. Trim off surplus pastry with a sharp knife, then knock up and flute edges with the back of knife. Brush top with milk or egg. Bake in preheated oven 200C, 400F, Gas Mark 6 for 30 minutes to set pastry, and then reduce heat to 180C, 350F, Gas Mark 4 for a further 10 minutes to set filling.

APRICOT AND PLUM FLAN

Of course we all know that fresh fruit is best, but when the fruit season has ended and we have to rely on dried, then soaking it in sherry or brandy will give it an extra kick, and it tastes just as good, well almost!

Serves 6.

Ingredients:
75g (3oz) butter
2 teaspoons caster sugar
150g (5oz) plain flour
Pinch of salt, & a little iced water

Filling:
225g (8oz) dried apricots
12 large prunes soaked in sherry &
  baked in a very slow oven (140C,
  275F, Gas Mark 1) with sufficient
  water to just cover.

Crumble butter into the sieved flour and mix with fingertips until it resembles fine breadcrumbs, add salt and sugar and mix with enough iced water (3-5 tablespoons) and make dough. Roll dough out on a floured surface and line a greased flan tin. Arrange the fruit in overlapping circles, making one circle with the stoned halved prunes and the rest with apricots. Sprinkle the fruit with sugar, but reserve juice. Put the flan on a baking sheet in the centre of preheated oven 200C, 400F, Gas Mark 6 and bake for 25-30 minutes. Reduce heat to 190C, 375F, Gas Mark 5 and bake for a further 10-15 minutes. Heat the juices left from the cooking of the fruit until they have formed a thick syrup. Pour this over the fruit and put back into the oven for another 5 minutes or so. This flan can be served hot or cold, or can be made an hour or two in advance and reheated in a low oven with a piece of buttered paper to cover the fruit. But do not be tempted to make fruit flans more than a few hours ahead of time, you will find the pastry becomes soggy with the fruit juice.

LEMON CAKE PIE

This recipe, which was given to me by an American friend, calls for an unbaked pastry shell. I use ready-made shortcrust pastry for quickness and make two, so that I can put one away in the freezer. I don't why it's called Lemon Cake Pie, but the name makes it sound a bit different to the more traditional Lemon Flan.

Serves 6.

Ingredients:

1 unbaked pastry shell or 225g (8oz) ready-made shortcrust pastry
225g (8oz) caster sugar
Grated rind and juice of 1 lemon

2 eggs separated
250ml (8fl oz) milk
10g (½oz) plain flour
10g (½oz) butter

If you are not using a ready-made pastry shell, roll out pastry on a floured surface and line a greased 20.5 (8 inch) flan tin. Set aside in fridge until required. Cream together the butter and sugar. Beat egg yolks and add flour, grated rind, lemon juice and milk. Beat egg whites until stiff and fold into mixture. Pour lemon mixture into pastry case and bake in preheated oven 220C, 425F, Gas Mark 7 for 10 minutes, then reduce heat to 170C, 325F, Gas Mark 3 for a further 25 minutes. Serve hot or cold.

CRUNCHY PEAR CRUMBLE

Fruit crumbles are so easy to prepare, and I tend to make them throughout the year as well as in the winter. The best thing about them is that you can use almost any fruit you choose to, or what's in season, and you have a delicious hot pudding, soft and fruity inside with a crunchy topping.

Serves 4-6.

Ingredients:	Topping:
900g (2lb) ripe pears	110g (4oz) plain flour
2 eggs	75g (3oz) butter
75g (3oz) caster sugar	50g (2oz) rolled oats
35g (1½oz) plain flour	25g (1oz) ground almonds
150ml (¼ pint) fromage frais	35g (1½oz) caster sugar
300ml (½ pint) milk	

Peel, core, and quarter pears and put in the bottom of buttered 1½ litre (2 pint) ovenproof dish. Beat eggs and sugar until light and fluffy, then beat in the flour and fromage frais. Gradually stir in the milk. Pour beaten mixture over the pears and bake in preheated oven 180C, 350F, Gas Mark 4 for 15 minutes. Meanwhile sift flour into mixing bowl and rub in the butter until mixture resembles breadcrumbs. Stir in the oats, ground almonds and sugar. Sprinkle over the partially cooked pears and bake for a further 20-25 minutes until the crumble is golden brown and the fruit juices bubble through. You can vary this pudding by adding 1 tablespoon chopped stem ginger, or using half pears and half apples, sprinkled with cinnamon.

PLUM COMPOTE

If you're counting calories, then this is the pudding for you. It takes only 20 minutes to assemble and is perfect to follow a heavy meal.

Serves 4-6.

Ingredients:

700g (1½lb) red plums, stoned & halved	Grated rind & juice of 1 large orange
1½ wine glasses of port	2 tablespoons redcurrant jelly
2 tablespoons sugar to taste	

Put all the ingredients, except the plums, in a pan and heat gently to melt the jelly. Add the plums cut side down and poach for about 12 minutes. Taste and add sugar if needed. Serve with homemade custard and sponge fingers.

RICH CHOCOLATE PUDDING *(With Fudge Sauce)*

This is one of my very old recipes, which I found tucked away in a notebook. It's a rich and filling sweet, and is always popular with children and adults alike.

Serves 4.

Ingredients:

75g (3oz) plain dark chocolate

175g (6oz) caster sugar

175g (6oz) butter

3 eggs

Fudge sauce:

225g (½lb) caramels

2 tablespoons milk

A few drops of vanilla essence

160g (5½oz) self-raising flour

10g (½oz) cocoa

150ml (¼ pint) milk

Grease a 1.5 litre (2½ pint) pudding basin. Break the chocolate into small pieces and place with the milk in small saucepan. Heat gently until melted and smooth. Leave to cool. Cream the butter and sugar together, adding the vanilla essence, until light and fluffy. Gradually beat in melted chocolate then beat in the whisked eggs a little at a time. Fold in sifted flour and cocoa. Turn the mixture into the prepared basin. Cover top of basin closely with double thickness of buttered greaseproof paper and tie down securely. Place in the top of a steamer and steam for 2 hours. Remove paper, turn pudding out onto a hot dish and pour a little of the prepared sauce over the top. Serve the remaining sauce in a small jug.

To prepare sauce: Place caramels into a small pan together with the milk and heat slowly until the caramels have melted. Stir well together and then pour into a serving jug.

WELSH CAKES

These cakes are delicious to eat straight from a hot griddle, sprinkled with caster sugar or spread with butter. I try to make enough to freeze, but they nearly always disappear as soon as they are cooked!

Makes about 16 cakes

Ingredients:

225g (8oz) self-raising flour

Pinch of mixed spice

50g (2oz) lard

1 egg, beaten

Pinch of salt

50g (2oz) margarine

75g (3oz) caster sugar

75g (3oz) mixed currants & sultanas

Sift flour, salt and mixed spice together. Rub margarine and lard into the mixture to resemble breadcrumbs. Add sugar and mixed fruit. Mix in beaten egg to form a soft dough. Roll out to 5mm (¼ inch) thick and cut into 5cm (2 inch) rounds. Grease a griddle or heavy based frying pan with a little lard, and when hot, fry cakes until lightly browned on both sides. Place on cooling tray to cool.

BANANA CHIFFON CAKE

This is a deliciously light cake, a real teatime treat, and one you will be asked to make again and again!

Ingredients:

200g (7oz) self-raising flour
Pinch of salt
¼ teaspoon cream of tartar
3 egg yolks
50ml (2fl oz) vegetable oil
½ teaspoon vanilla essence

2 teaspoons baking powder
4 egg whites
1 medium sized banana, peeled
75ml (3fl oz) cold water
175g (6oz) caster sugar

Sieve together the flour, salt and baking powder. Beat together the egg whites and cream of tartar until it forms soft peaks. Chop up the banana in a blender, then drop in the egg yolks, water, oil, sugar and vanilla essence, and blend for 30 seconds. Scrape down the sides of the goblet and blend for a further 10 seconds. Pour the mixture gently into the bowl of flour and stir until smooth. Then fold the flour mixture into the egg whites. Turn into two greased and lined sandwich tins and bake at 170C, 325F, Gas Mark 3 for 30 minutes or until the cakes feel firm in the middle. Turn the cakes out gently onto a cooling rack and leave to cool. Sandwich them together with butter cream or fresh whipped cream. Dredge the top of cake with icing sugar.

MAPLE, WALNUT AND RAISIN BISCUITS

These biscuits make a good lunch-box filler, you can vary the ingredients by substituting the raisins for apricots or white chocolate broken into small pieces.

Makes 18.

Ingredients:

225g (8oz) butter
2 eggs beaten
225g (8oz) chopped walnuts
1 teaspoon vanilla essence

175g (6oz) soft, light brown sugar
275g (9½oz) self-raising flour
110g (4oz) raisins
6 tablespoons maple syrup

Cream together the butter and sugar until light and fluffy. Gradually beat in the eggs until fully incorporated, then stir in the flour, nuts, raisins or chocolate, vanilla essence and maple syrup. Spoon 18 teaspoons of mixture, spaced well apart, on a greased baking sheet. Bake at 190C, 375F, Gas Mark 5 for 15 minutes or until golden brown. Cool on a wire tray. Store in an airtight tin.

CHERRY AND APRICOT SCONES

These make a change from fruit or plain scones, and can be toasted if they get a bit stale, and again I always make a large batch so that I can freeze some.

Makes about 18-20

Ingredients:

450g (1lb) plain flour
1 teaspoon bicarbonate of soda
50g (2oz) caster sugar
225ml (8fl oz) milk

2 teaspoons cream of tartar
110g (4oz) butter
75g (3oz) cherries, chopped
75g (3oz) no-need to soak dried
    apricots, chopped

Sift together the flour, cream of tartar and bicarbonate of soda. Rub in the butter until mixture resembles fine breadcrumbs. Stir in the sugar, chopped cherries and apricots, mix well. Stir in enough milk to give a fairly soft dough. Turn onto a lightly floured surface, knead lightly and roll out to about 2cm (¾ inch) thickness. Cut into 6cm (2½ inch) rounds with a cutter. Place on baking sheet and bake in preheated oven 230C, 450F, Gas Mark 8 for 10-15 minutes. Roll out remaining dough and repeat the process.

PICKLED ONIONS

If you pickle your onions now you will have them ready for Christmas!

Ingredients:

1.35kg (3lb) pickling onions, peeled
10 peppercorns
12 allspice berries
1½ litres (2 pints) distilled malt vinegar

225g (8oz) sea salt
4 blades of mace
5cm (2 inch) cinnamon stick

Place onions in a bowl. Combine 2.25 litres (4 pints) water and salt together. Pour over the onions, cover with a large plate to keep them submerged for at least 36 hours. Drain the onions, rinse well and pack into clean jars. Add the spices, top up with vinegar, seal and leave for at least 3 months before opening.

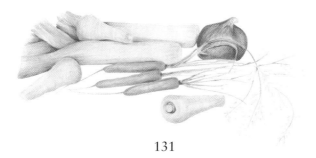

Contents – November

November

Some say that November is a sad month, but with all the activity that goes on in my kitchen during the month before Christmas I would say it's anything but sad. It's the month when we traditionally should make our Christmas puddings, and begin to make lists of things we will need for Christmas, and I usually order my turkey in November from a local farm. And if I've any Seville oranges left in my freezer from last January, I set to and make some more marmalade. It's useful to have some spare pots just before Christmas so that they maybe given to local bazaars or fund raiser stalls in the village, and the kitchen is the best place to be on a cold winter's day – I find a good baking session will soon blow away those November blues.

BACON, CARROT & CORIANDER SOUP

A delicious and colourful soup, which has a creamy texture and flavour, and the added bonus of being low in calories!

Serves 4.

Ingredients:

450g (1lb) carrots, peeled & finely chopped
2 tablespoons fresh coriander, roughly chopped
6 lean streaky rashers of bacon, diced
3 lean streaky rashers of bacon, grilled until crispy

700ml (1¼ pints) ham stock
1 teaspoon dried coriander leaves
110g (4oz) low-fat crème fraiche
1 large onion, finely chopped
150ml (¼ pint) white wine
Salt & black pepper

Dry fry the 6 rashers of bacon for 2-3 minutes, add onion and carrots to the pan and sauté for a further 3 minutes. Add the stock, wine and dried herbs. Season well and simmer for 10-15 minutes until carrots are soft. Blend until smooth using either a liquidiser or food processor. Stir in the crème fraiche and fresh coriander and season to taste. Serve sprinkled with the crispy bacon and wedges of crusty bread.

VEGETABLE SOUP

This soup is a meal in itself, especially if you have some crusty wholemeal rolls to serve with it.

Serves 6-8.

Ingredients:

3 large onions, peeled & sliced
1 turnip, peeled & chopped
25g (1oz) butter or margarine
850ml (1½ pints) chicken stock or water

3 parsnips, peeled & chopped
2 leeks, cleaned & chopped
450g (1lb) carrots, peeled & chopped

Melt butter or margarine in a large saucepan, add chopped vegetables and stir with a wooden spoon so that the vegetables absorb the fat. Add stock or water so that the vegetables are well covered. Season lightly with salt and pepper. Simmer until vegetables are soft, about an hour. Liquidise or sieve. Season to taste. This soup freezes very well after which it may be necessary to thin with stock, water or milk. Garnish with parsley or croutons.

TOMATO FISH BAKE

A tasty supper dish, or you can serve it for lunch with buttered cabbage or leeks.

Serves 4.

Ingredients:

50g (2oz) fresh breadcrumbs
½ teaspoon mixed herbs
450g (1lb) white fish
50g (2oz) mushrooms, sliced
2 level tablespoons tomato purée
¼ teaspoon of sugar
1 small onion, peeled & finely chopped
300ml (½ pint) milk, plus
  2-3 tablespoons

50g (2oz) Cheddar cheese, grated
Salt and pepper
25g (1oz) butter
25g (1oz) flour
1 teaspoon lemon juice
450g (1lb) potatoes, peeled
Parsley or watercress to garnish

Make a stuffing with breadcrumbs, cheese, onion, herbs, seasoning and 2-3 tablespoons of milk. Wash and skin fish. Place half on the base of a buttered shallow ovenproof dish. Spread stuffing over and top with remaining fish. Melt butter in a saucepan and fry mushrooms until soft. Add flour, remaining 300ml (½ pint) milk, tomato purée, lemon juice, sugar and seasoning. Heat, whisking until it thickens. Pour over fish. Bake in preheated oven 190C, 375F, Gas Mark 5 for 25 minutes. Meanwhile boil potatoes and mash with a little milk. Remove fish from oven and pipe mashed potato as a border round the dish. Return to oven, or grill until brown, garnish.

SMOKED TROUT PATÉ

If you want to make a quick starter for a dinner party, or want to have something that's a bit different for a sandwich filling, then this paté is ideal, it's put together in a few minutes and will keep covered in your fridge for two days.

Serves 6.

Ingredients:

4 smoked trout fillets
225g (8oz) soft, creamed butter
2 teaspoons horseradish sauce

2 tablespoons lemon juice
50g (2oz) double cream

Thoroughly blend trout and butter together in a mixing bowl, I usually use my hand mixer, but if you're feeling energetic you can mix it with a wooden spoon. Gradually mix in the cream, lemon juice and horseradish sauce, season well. Chill for several hours and serve with thin slices of toast.

SAUSAGE AND BACON RISOTTO

This is a low fat, but robust meal which I often serve for dinner or lunch, it's quite substantial and filling, and just what is needed on a cold November day.

Serves 4.

Ingredients:

4 very lean rashers of streaky bacon, cut into small pieces
275g (10oz) risotto rice
2 x 400g (14oz) cans of chopped tomatoes
425ml (¾ pint) vegetable stock (cube will do)

8 low fat sausages, cut into quarters
1 large onion, peeled & chopped
2 teaspoons paprika
4 teaspoons fresh (if dried, use less) basil roughly chopped
Salt & black pepper

Dry fry sausage, bacon and onion for 2-3 minutes in a wok or non-stick frying pan. Add rice and all the remaining ingredients. Bring to the boil, cover and simmer for 20 minutes, giving an occasional stir. If too wet, remove lid for last 5 minutes. Serve with crusty bread and a mixed salad.

COTTAGE PIE WITH CRISPY LEEK & POTATO TOPPING

Adding leeks and cheese to the potato topping makes it less bland, and you can use pork or lamb instead of beef. If you've any meat left over from your Sunday joint then use this minced, and add a tin of butter beans to give more bulk.

Serves 4.

Ingredients:
450g (1lb) minced beef
1 large onion, peeled & chopped
2 carrots, peeled & chopped
2 tablespoons plain flour
300ml (½ pint) beef cube stock
1 tablespoon tomato purée
1 tablespoon mixed dried herbs
Salt & pepper

Leek & potato topping:
700g (1½lb) potatoes, peeled & chopped
2 leeks, sliced
Knob of butter
50g (2oz) Cheddar cheese, grated
Salt & black pepper

Boil the potatoes, until softened, adding leeks 5 minutes before the end. Meanwhile, dry fry the mince, onion and carrots for 4-5 minutes. Add the flour. Gradually add stock, tomato purée and dried herbs. Bring to the boil and stir until thickened. Season and transfer to ovenproof dish. Drain and mash potatoes and leeks with butter and half the cheese. Season. Place on top of mince mixture. Sprinkle with remaining cheese. Bake in preheated oven 190C, 375F, Gas Mark 5 for 25-30 minutes until golden. Serve with Brussels sprouts or buttered cabbage.

MY EASY LASAGNE

I've given this recipe to countless friends in the past, and thought I ought to include it in my book. It's a dish that really doesn't need any vegetables to accompany it, except perhaps a green salad and some crusty bread to mop up the juices.

Serves 4.

Ingredients:
450g (1lb) lean minced beef, or
    lamb, or pork
425ml (¾ pint) passata or
    creamed tomatoes
1 medium onion, peeled & chopped
1 meat stock cube
Salt and black pepper
8-10 sheets 'no cook' lasagne pasta

1 clove garlic, crushed
1 teaspoon dried herbs
280g (10oz) frozen spinach, thawed
1 medium egg
150ml (¼ pint) skimmed milk
50g (2 oz) cheese, grated
150g (5oz) low-fat natural yoghurt

Dry fry minced beef, onion and garlic until browned. Add passata or creamed tomatoes, crumbled stock cube and herbs, season and simmer for 10 minutes. Lightly squeeze spinach. Layer into ovenproof dish, meat first, top with sheets of lasagne pasta, then spinach, pasta and finally meat mixture. Whisk egg, yoghurt and milk together, stir in half of the cheese. Spoon over meat to cover it completely. Sprinkle with remaining cheese. Bake for 25-30 minutes in preheated oven 180C, 350F, Gas Mark 4 until golden brown.

POTATO AND BLUE CHEESE GRATIN

I sometimes end up with a wedge of blue cheese in my fridge and generally use it in a quiche or sprinkled on soup, but in this recipe I've used it instead of Cheddar cheese. It gives a delicious creamy flavour to the gratin and makes a substantial winter's day lunch or supper served with a side salad.

Serves 8 (or 4, halving the ingredients).

Ingredients:

700g (1½lb) potatoes, peeled, rinsed well & sliced thin (make sure to pat dry)

2 large onions, peeled & sliced thin

425ml-600ml (¾-1 pint) milk

225g (8oz) turnips, peeled & thinly sliced

2 teaspoons chopped fresh or dried thyme

75g (3oz) blue cheese, crumbled

4 large egg yolks

1 large garlic clove, halved

25g (1oz) unsalted butter

3 tablespoons crème fraiche

Salt & black pepper to taste

Rub the insides of a very large deep baking dish, at least 2¼ litres (4 pints), with the cut side of garlic clove, and butter the dish. Layer the vegetables, seasoning each layer with salt and pepper, and a little thyme. In a bowl mash together the cheese, crème fraiche and egg yolks. Gradually whisk the milk. Pour cheese mixture over the potatoes. Dot with butter and bake, covered with foil, for 45 minutes in preheated oven 190C, 375F, Gas Mark 5 for 45 minutes. Uncover and bake for another 15 minutes, or until potatoes are tender and top is golden brown.

BEEF AND BEAN HOTPOT

A hot nourishing dish to make on a cold winter's day, which you can serve either with jacket potatoes, or for a cheese topping, take about 175g (6oz) potatoes mixed with 50g (2oz) Cheddar cheese, a knob of butter, a little cheese sprinkled on top and garnished with parsley.

Serves 4.

Ingredients:

450g (1lb) lean beef
1 onion, sliced
2 teaspoons paprika
Salt & black pepper
1 x 400g (14oz) can chopped tomatoes
1 x 400g (14oz) can mixed beans, kidney, chick beans, etc.

1 tablespoon oil
1 tablespoon plain flour
1 teaspoon mild chilli powder
150ml (¼ pint) red wine
2 sticks of celery, sliced
1 red pepper, deseeded & chopped
2 carrots, peeled & sliced

Heat oil in a large pan, and fry onion until soft. Add the meat and cook for 5 minutes until browned. Mix the flour with the spices. Add to the pan then stir in the wine and tomatoes. Add the beans, carrots, celery and pepper, and slowly bring to the boil. Simmer for 1½ hours in preheated oven 180C, 350F, Gas Mark 4. Serve with jacket potatoes and green vegetables, or the topping I have given above.

WINTER PUDDING

This is a large family pudding, and provided you have a light main course you will be able to tuck into a generous helping of it!

Serves 6-8.

Ingredients:

350g (12oz) self-raising flour
175g (6oz) shredded suet
175g (6oz) sultanas
75g (3oz) 'ready to eat' dried apricots, chopped
1 large egg, beaten
Pinch of salt

75g (3oz) chopped dates
½ level teaspoon ground ginger
1 medium sized carrot, peeled
1 level teaspoon ground cinnamon
75g (3oz) granulated sugar
Milk to mix

Place all the dry ingredients into a mixing bowl. Grate carrot as finely as possible, add to the bowl and mix together thoroughly. Add egg and mix with enough milk to make a soft consistency. Turn into a large well greased pudding basin, cover with greased paper or foil and steam for 2½-3 hours. Turn out on serving plate and serve with hot homemade custard.

HOMEMADE CUSTARD

If you want REAL custard, then nothing beats homemade. To make a really rich custard, cream is used, but I always use milk as I think the egg yolks are sufficient to give a creamy texture.

Serves 6–8.

Ingredients:

1 egg yolk & 4 eggs	2 teaspoon cornflour
1½ tablespoons caster sugar	600ml (1 pint) milk

Blend eggs and egg yolk with cornflour and sugar. Heat milk to just below boiling point, then stir in the egg liquid. Rinse the milk saucepan. Return the mixture to the rinsed saucepan and cook over a very slow heat, stirring constantly until custard thickens. Pour into a cool basin and cover the surface with greaseproof paper until needed.

CHRISTMAS PUDDING 1.

I always try to make my Christmas puddings in November, and by using breadcrumbs you get a lighter pudding. I make one large pudding for Christmas Day, and use the same recipe to make 2 smaller ones – one to keep for Easter and the other to give away.

Serves 6-8.

Ingredients:

225g (8oz) raisins	350g (12oz) fine white breadcrumbs
225g (8oz) currants	225g (8oz) suet
225g (8oz) sultanas	110g (4oz) mixed chopped glacé peel
1 grated carrot	1 grated small apple
225g (8oz) soft brown sugar	35g (1½oz) blanched almonds
½ juice & grated zest of l lemon	½ teaspoon nutmeg
½ teaspoon salt	2 teaspoons allspice
4 large fresh eggs	300ml (½ pint) beer or stout

Stir all the ingredients together thoroughly, if mixture is not quite wet enough, add a little milk. Put the mixture into a greased 900g (2lb) pudding basin and tie down with greaseproof paper and foil paper. Steam for 6-8 hours. Take off the covers and allow the pudding to dry out well, then cover with clean dry paper or cloth. Store the pudding in a cool place and steam for a further 2 hours on Christmas Day or on the day you are going to eat it. Serve with brandy butter or custard.

CHRISTMAS PUDDING 2. *(with chocolate)!*

Although I usually make the traditional Christmas pudding each year, I have tried this recipe, and find that adding chocolate really does make a subtle difference to the pudding, and enhances its flavour. This year I will be making 4 small ones from this recipe – one to keep and eat, and three to give away as presents, labelling them 'Chocolate Christmas Pudding' to keep the lucky recipients guessing!

Serves 6.

Ingredients:

175g (6oz) plain flour
½ teaspoon grated nutmeg
110g (4oz) shredded suet
110g (4oz) currants
225g (8oz) sultanas
Grated zest of 1 lemon
2 eggs, beaten
75g (3oz) good quality plain
  chocolate, chopped

1 teaspoon mixed spice
75g (3oz) fresh brown breadcrumbs
110g (4oz) raisins
110g (4oz) chopped stoned dates
1 large apple grated
75g (3oz) dark brown sugar
300ml (½ pint) stout

Sift flour and spices into a mixing bowl. Add breadcrumbs, suet, dried fruits, apple, sugar, peel and chocolate. Mix together and gradually stir in eggs and stout. Leave mixture covered, overnight. Turn into a greased 1½ litre (2 pint) pudding basin, and cover with greased paper and a pudding cloth. Steam for 6 hours. Re-steam for 2 hours before serving with hot rum sauce.

SPECIAL RICE PUDDING

For those who don't like rice pudding, this one will make them change their minds, and it's a good way of getting children to eat it.

Serves 4.

Ingredients:

35g (1½oz) pudding rice	600ml (1 pint) milk
50g (2oz) caster sugar	1 large egg & two egg yolks beaten
150ml (¼ pint) double cream	110g (4oz) dried apricots soaked overnight in brandy

Simmer rice with the sugar in the milk over a very low heat for about 35 minutes, stirring occasionally to prevent the rice sticking, until the rice is soft and cooked. Leave to cool a little. Then beat in the eggs and cream and the apricots, sliced. Pour into a buttered dish and bake in a preheated oven 180C, 350F, Gas Mark 4 for about 25 minutes. Meanwhile beat the two remaining egg whites until stiff and then fold in 110g (4oz) caster sugar, pile on top of the rice and bake for a further 10-15 minutes until the meringue is crisp and set.

JAM ROLY POLY

This is another popular pudding that just has to be served with real homemade custard.

Serves 6.

Ingredients:

350g (12oz) plain flour	2 rounded teaspoons baking powder
175g (6oz) finely chopped suet	Pinch of salt
Jam	Water to mix

Sift the flour and baking powder, add the suet and salt. Mix with sufficient water to make a soft, but firm, dough. Roll it into a rectangle about 5mm (¼ inch) thick. Spread with jam almost to the edge. Damp the edges and roll up lightly. Seal the edges. Wrap the pudding in a scalded, well-floured cloth, and tie up the ends. Put into fast boiling water and simmer for 2-2½ hours. Turn out on a serving plate.

APPLE CAP PUDDING

This is a very old Somerset recipe that was given to me when I first got married. Since then it has been adapted in lots of different versions, but I like this one best.

Serves 4.

Ingredients:
1 large cooking apple
25g (1oz) caster sugar
10g (½oz) butter
Squeeze of half a lemon

For the cap:
110g (4oz) self-raising flour
50g (2oz) butter
50g (2oz) caster sugar
Grated rind of l lemon
1 large egg
Milk to mix

Butter an 850ml (1½ pint) pudding basin. Peel, core, quarter and slice the apple thinly. Lay the slices in the bottom of the basin, adding the sugar, remaining butter and lemon juice.

To make the cap: Place the flour and sugar into a mixing bowl. Rub in the butter and mix in the lemon rind. Add the beaten egg and enough milk to make a soft mixture. Place this on top of the apple, cover with buttered paper or foil. Steam for 2 hours. Turn out the pudding and serve hot with custard sauce.

FUDGE PIE

The ingredients given in this recipe make quite a large pie, so if you are serving less than 8 portions halve the ingredients. It's a delicious treat, especially for the sweet-toothed and for those who occasionally enjoy a really rich dessert!

Serves 8-10.

Ingredients:
175g (6oz) plain flour
Pinch of salt
75g (3oz) butter

For the filling:
175g (6oz) butter
175g (6oz) soft light brown sugar
1 x 400g (14oz) condensed milk
50g (2oz) chopped walnuts
50g (2oz) seedless raisins

Sift flour and salt into a mixing bowl, rub in butter to a firm consistency with a little iced cold water. Roll out the pastry and line a greased and lined round 20.5 cm (8 inch) or square 18cm (7 inch) cake tin, trimming the edges and crimping them neatly. Line the pastry with rice or beans and bake blind in preheated oven 200C, 400F, Gas Mark 6 for 15-20 minutes, remove the weighting and return pastry to oven for a further few minutes until golden brown and crisp. Carefully turn out onto a wire tray to cool. Put the butter, soft brown sugar and condensed milk into a heavy based saucepan and melt over a very gentle heat, being careful not to boil, until all the sugar has dissolved. Then bring to the boil and boil steadily for about 6 minutes, stirring continually. Take off the heat and stir in the chopped walnuts and raisins, then pour mixture into the cooked pastry case. Leave to cool and set. Serve on its own, or with a little single cream.

APRICOT AND GINGER CRUMBLE

As the winter progresses, I think we tend to eat more warming food, and this crumble is one of the nicest hot puddings I make from time to time, real comfort food!

Serves 6.

Ingredients:
2 x 425g (15oz) tins apricot
    halves in fruit juice
2 cooking apples, peeled,
    cored & diced
35g (1½oz) granulated sugar

For the crumble:
50g (2oz) butter
110g (4 oz) plain flour
75g (3oz) soft brown sugar
½ level teaspoon ground ginger
1½ litre (2 pint) ovenproof dish

Put one tin of the apricot halves and juice into ovenproof dish. Drain the contents of the other tin and put this fruit also into the dish. Sprinkle the diced apples over the top. Add the sugar and press it into the liquid. Rub the butter into the flour, sugar and ginger until it resembles fine breadcrumbs, and sprinkle this over the top of the fruit. Bake in preheated oven at 190C, 375F, Gas Mark 5 for 25-30 minutes, until cooked through and lightly golden. This goes well served with vanilla ice-cream.

COFFEE CRUNCH CAKE

Although this recipe is really a cake to be served at tea-time or with coffee, you can serve it warmed with fromage frais for dessert.

Serves 4-6.

Ingredients:
110g (4oz) self-raising flour
1 teaspoon baking powder
110g (4oz) butter, at room temperature
110g (4oz) soft light brown sugar
2 eggs, beaten
1 tablespoon instant coffee mixed
with 1 tablespoon water

For the topping:
50g (2oz) plain flour
50g (2oz) demerara sugar
2 teaspoons quality instant coffee
    granules & 25g (1oz) butter

Sift flour and baking powder together in a mixing bowl, add butter, sugar, eggs and instant coffee and beat all together until well mixed. Put this into a greased 20.5 (8 inch) cake tin and set aside. With a mixer (or a fork) work the butter into the flour for the topping and make it like breadcrumbs. Mix in the sugar and instant coffee granules. Spoon this over the cake mixture and bake in a preheated oven at 180C, 350F, Gas Mark 4 for 30 minutes. Cool on wire rack and serve dredged with icing sugar.

ONE-STAGE FRUITY ROCK CAKES

These are a good standby if you want to have something in your cake tin to go with a cup of tea when friends drop in unexpectedly.

Makes 10-12

Ingredients:
225g (8oz) self-raising flour
110g (4oz) soft margarine
1 standard egg
75g (3oz) caster sugar

½ level teaspoon baking powder
110g (4oz) mixed dried fruit & peel
1 tablespoon milk

Place all ingredients in a mixing bowl and beat together for 2-3 minutes. Place heaped teaspoons of the mixture well apart on baking sheets, previously brushed with oil or melted margarine. Bake in preheated oven 200C, 400F, Gas Mark 6 on second and third shelves from top of oven for 15-20 minutes. Remove and cool on wire tray.

APRICOT AND MARMALADE SLICES

This is a shortbread type of dough with an unusual texture. It's given a tart marmalade centre with a grated topping from the remaining dough.

Makes 12

Ingredients:
175g (6oz) butter, softened
60g (2½oz) caster sugar
1½ tablespoons vegetable oil
½ teaspoon vanilla essence
1 medium egg
350g (12oz) plain flour
½ teaspoon baking powder

Filling:
225g (8oz) thick-cut orange marmalade
75g (3oz) ready-to-eat apricots, chopped
Grated rind of half 1 small orange
1 tablespoon orange juice
20g (¾oz) toasted almond flakes
Little icing sugar for dusting

Cream the butter and sugar together until soft and creamy, then beat in the oil followed by the vanilla essence and egg. Sift together the flour and baking powder and gradually work into the mixture until blended. Line a small Swiss roll tin with greased greaseproof paper. Combine the marmalade, chopped apricots, orange rind and juice together. Use just under half the dough and press it evenly to cover the tin, and then spread evenly with the marmalade mixture. Using a coarse grater, grate the remaining dough over the fruit mixture. Sprinkle with almonds and bake in a preheated oven at 150C, 300F, Gas Mark 2 for about 40 minutes or until golden and the topping set. Remove from the oven and leave to cool in the tin. Cover with foil and leave in tin for 24 hours (this is necessary). Then dredge lightly with icing sugar and cut into fingers or squares. Will store in an airtight tin for up to 8 days, or freeze for up to 3 months.

CHERRY BISCUITS

These dainty little biscuits are easy for children to make and will keep them occupied during the school holidays!

Makes about 12.

Ingredients:
175g (6oz) plain flour
50g (2oz) cornflour
2 tablespoons icing sugar
175g (6oz) butter

Icing:
110g (4oz) icing sugar
1 egg white, beaten
Glacé cherries

146

Rub butter into dry ingredients. Roll out thinly on a floured surface and cut into 24 rounds with a 5cm (2 inch) pastry cutter. Bake in a preheated oven 180C, 350F, Gas Mark 4 for about 10 minutes. Cool on a wire tray, then put two biscuits together with raspberry jam and ice top with glacé icing, and decorate each biscuit with half a glacé cherry.

Contents – December

December

In East Anglia where I live we get the most beautiful sunsets, especially on those clear, bitterly cold evenings when the sun goes down almost as though it's in flames, lighting up the sky and casting red and deep pink colours onto cottage walls and windows. Shops are beginning to look festive and Christmassy, our main High Street is lit up with coloured lights, and at night the village looks like a picture from a Christmas fairytale book, with the lights shining into the December darkness. Planning and preparation now starts in earnest, but we still have to eat before the Christmas Day feast begins, so soups are high on my list this month, and I've included three thick nourishing ones in this chapter. Remember, root vegetables store better in the winter if they are unscrubbed, and there is a variety of crunchy winter salads you can make using crisp cabbage, celery, beetroot, apples and chicory.

By now I will have made my Christmas pudding, and cake, which I shall marzipan and ice a week before Christmas and if, like me, you've remembered to order your turkey well in advance for Christmas, you will now only have the trimmings and last minute preparations to worry about!

149

PASTA AND BEAN SOUP

This is one of most satisfying and nourishing soups I make, and I serve it often during the winter months. It's a meal in itself and really doesn't need anything to accompany it, not even a crusty roll, but perhaps a slice of crusty bread to mop up the juices!

Serves 4.

Ingredients:

1 tablespoon olive oil	2 medium onions, peeled & chopped
2 garlic cloves, crushed	225g (8oz) cooked haricot beans
50g (2oz) dried pasta shapes	1½ litres (2 pints) chicken cube stock
1 green pepper, deseeded & chopped	Salt & pepper
4 ripe tomatoes, peeled, chopped	1 dessertspoon pesto or fresh
& deseeded	chopped basil (dried will do)

Heat oil in large saucepan and cook onion, garlic, pepper and tomatoes for a few minutes. Pour on the stock and bring to the boil. Then simmer to reduce by about 300ml (½ pint). Pour a little of the liquid into a blender with about 75g (3oz) of the cooked beans and make a purée. Add this and the rest of the beans to the soup and bring back to the boil. Add the pasta and cook till it is 'al dente'. Season to taste and add a dessertspoonful of pesto, it gives the soup a lovely flavour, or if you've none in stock, add some chopped fresh or dried basil. Serve piping hot.

THICK ONION AND POTATO SOUP

I use potatoes in this soup to thicken it, instead of cornflour, as I find the soup reheats better and is not so solid, but if you prefer to thicken it with cornflour instead of potatoes the soup will taste just as good, but you will need to add extra liquid if you reheat it.

Serves 4.

Ingredients:

450g (1lb) onions, peeled & sliced	3 large potatoes, peeled & sliced
1 teaspoon dry mustard	A knob of butter or dripping
1½ litres (2 pints) chicken stock	Salt & pepper to taste
(cube will do)	

Melt the fat in a large frying pan. Fry the onions and potato lightly for about 10 minutes, taking care not to brown them. Add the salt and pepper. Meanwhile heat chicken stock in a saucepan, then add contents of frying pan and bring to the boil.

Simmer for about 25 minutes, and serve very hot. If you have a 'head cold' this will help to cure it!

CARROT AND GINGER SOUP

The fresh ginger, curry and carrots make a really aromatic and colourful soup to serve in the wintertime.

Serves 6.

Ingredients:

6 tablespoons vegetable oil
4 garlic cloves, crushed
200ml (⅓ pint) dry white wine
2 tablespoons lemon juice
Salt & pepper to taste

1 large onion, peeled & chopped
1½ litres (2 pints) chicken stock cube
700g (1½lb) carrots, peeled & chopped
Pinch of curry powder
25g (1oz) finely chopped fresh ginger root

Melt the oil in a large saucepan over a gentle heat. Add onion, garlic and ginger and fry lightly for about 20 minutes, but do not brown onion. Add stock, wine and carrots and heat to boiling point. Then reduce heat and simmer, covered, until carrots are cooked, takes about 35 minutes. Put into blender or food processor and purée. Add salt and pepper, lemon juice and curry powder. Serve piping hot with wedges of wholemeal bread.

GARLIC MUSHROOMS

When you haven't got time to make a fussy or elaborate starter, you'll find this one is easy to assemble, and it doesn't take long to cook.

Serves 4.

Ingredients:

120g (4½oz) mushrooms
150ml (¼ pint) whipping cream
110g (4oz) cream cheese with
  garlic & herbs

5 rashers of streaky bacon, chopped
A little vegetable oil

Heat oil in a frying pan and fry bacon until crisp. Chop the mushrooms and add to the bacon. When cooked, mix in the cream cheese and enough whipping cream to make a thick sauce. Divide the mixture between 4 ramekins and place a thin slice of mushroom on top of each one. Place under a hot grill and heat through, browning slightly before serving.

TUNA MOULDS

A starter which is equally good for a light lunch served with crusty bread, and its quick and easy to assemble.

Serves 4 for a starter, or 2 for lunch.

Ingredients:

2 x 200g (7oz) tins of tuna
2 tablespoons capers
½ cup (breakfast size) chives
½ onion, chopped

2 hard boiled eggs, peeled & chopped
1 cup (breakfast size) mayonnaise
1 Packet gelatine dissolved in ½ cup
    boiling water

Drain liquid from the tins of tuna. Combine all the ingredients thoroughly and press into a dish or individual dishes and leave to set. Serve garnished with salad leaves.

SPICY RICE AND PRAWN SUPPER DISH

A spicy meal that is satisfying and a bit different. You can vary the ingredients, adding chopped chicken instead of ham, and putting strips of omelette on top of the rice makes an unusual and colourful garnish.

Serves 4.

Ingredients:

280g (10oz) cooked rice
50g (2oz) butter
½ teaspoon chilli
1 clove garlic
2 eggs
Salt & pepper

110g (4oz) chopped ham
1 chopped onion
2 teaspoons ground coriander
110g (4oz) prawns
1 tablespoon milk

Melt 25g (1oz) butter in a frying pan and cook the onion. Add the coriander, chilli and chopped garlic. Cook for 4-5 minutes slowly. Add the ham and prawns, stir in the rice and rest of the butter. Set aside and keep warm. Make an omelette with the eggs and milk, cut into strips and serve on top of the rice as garnish.

CREAMED FRESH HADDOCK AND ALMONDS

This dish is similar to a fish pie without the potatoes, so you can serve it with either mashed potatoes or homemade potato scallops.

Serves 6.

Ingredients:

700g (1½lb) fresh haddock
1 tablespoon plain flour
600ml (1 pint) water
2 tablespoons cream
1 tablespoon chopped parsley

35g (1½oz) butter
1 tablespoon grated cheese
Salt & pepper
1 tablespoon dry white wine
10g (½oz) almonds, blanched &
  roughly chopped

Cook haddock in boiling, salted water for about 15 minutes. Remove fish, set aside and keep warm. Keep stock for sauce. Melt butter in pan, add flour and cheese, and stir well, adding fish stock gradually, simmer until it thickens and bubbles. Season and remove from heat. Add the cream, wine and parsley. Remove skin and bones from the cooked fish and put it into a mixing bowl, and try not to break up the fish too much, it should be in large lumps. Pour over the sauce, mix carefully and put into an ovenproof dish, sprinkle with the chopped almonds and cook in preheated oven 180C, 350F, Gas Mark 4 for 15 minutes. If the almonds have not browned, finish off under a hot grill for a few minutes. Serve piping hot.

CHEESE AND ONION PLAIT

This makes an excellent main course, served hot with a jacket potato and creamed carrots. I make it throughout the year, especially if I am cooking for a large number of people, when I make several to serve cold with bowls of salad on the buffet table.

Serves 4.

Ingredients:

225g (8oz) frozen puff pastry
25g (1oz) butter
150ml (¼ pint) milk
2 tablespoons Parmesan cheese

3 medium sized onions
1 teaspoon cornflour
110g (4oz) Cheddar cheese, grated
Salt & pepper

Peel and chop onions. Cook gently in butter. Mix cornflour in a little milk and add to onions with the remainder of the milk and stir until thickened. Add grated cheese and Parmesan. Season with salt and pepper. Set aside to cool. Meanwhile, roll out pastry to an oblong – about 35cm x 25.5cm (14" x 10"). Then make diagonal cuts from edges halfway to middle through both thicknesses of pastry. Open out and place on greased baking tray. Spread cheese and onion mixture down middle of pastry. Fold cut strips alternately across filling. Bake in preheated oven 200C, 400F, Gas Mark 6 until the pastry is cooked through and golden brown. Eat hot or cold.

CHICKEN PIE

This pie tastes good eaten hot or cold, and the stock from cooking the fowl makes excellent soup.

Serves 4.

Ingredients:
300g (10½oz) plain flour
50g (2oz) lard
50g (2oz) margarine
Cold water to mix

Filling:
Half a 1.6kg (3½lb) boiling fowl
1 tin condensed mushroom soup
Chopped parsley
Pinch of salt

Boil the fowl for about 2½ hours until cooked. When it has cooled a little, cut half the meat into cubes (you can either make two pies or use the other half of the chicken for curry etc.) Meanwhile put flour, lard and margarine into a mixing bowl and rub fats into flour with fingertips until it resembles fine breadcrumbs. Mix to a firm dough with cold water and leave to rest for about 30 minutes in fridge. Sprinkle flour on a floured pastry board or work surface, and roll ⅔ of the pastry out to fit a 20.5cm (8 inch) pie dish. Mix cubed chicken and soup together (do not add liquid to the condensed soup) and put into pastry case with parsley. Roll out remaining pastry for the lid and place on top. Brush lid with beaten egg or milk and bake in preheated oven 200C, 400F, Gas Mark 6 for 45 minutes. Serve with creamed potatoes and green vegetable.

FARMHOUSE CASSEROLE

A lovely warming dish with all the goodness of the vegetables and herbs, making a robust and substantial dish to serve on a cold December day. I sometimes use best neck of lamb instead of beef, which is just as good.

Serves 4-6.

Ingredients:
900g (2lb) skirt of beef, thickly sliced
4 medium onions, peeled & chopped
225g (8oz) button mushrooms
300ml (½ pint) light ale
1 extra bay leaf
2 tablespoons tomato paste

4 large carrots, peeled & chopped
450g (1lb) tomatoes
1 stick celery, chopped
50g (2oz) butter
Seasoning to taste
Bouquet garni (thyme, parsley & bay leaf, tied in a bunch)

Melt butter in heavy based pan and quickly fry beef, browning on all sides. Then set aside to keep warm, and lightly fry onion, celery, carrots and mushrooms. When all are soft, put into a large casserole with the beef. Cover with the ale and stir in tomato paste. Season well and add the bouquet garni and bay leaf. Cover and cook in preheated oven 180C, 350F, Gas Mark 4 for 2½-3 hours. Serve with creamed potatoes and broccoli.

SPICED BEEF

Spiced Beef is a change from cold turkey at Christmas time, and it's useful to have a piece ready to cut out for sandwiches or eat with a salad or a main meal with sauté potatoes – delicious!

Serves approximately 8-10.

Ingredients:

1.8kg (4lb) brisket of beef, rolled & secured with meat skewers (your butcher will do this for you)	4 tablespoons salt 4 tablespoons pickling spice, including a piece of stem ginger, tied up in muslin

Put the beef joint into a large saucepan, add the salt, and then the spice and ginger in muslin. Cover with cold water and bring to the boil. Simmer gently for 3-4 hours. Remove from hotplate and let the joint remain in the liquid until it's quite cold. It's then ready to serve.

ROAST TURKEY WITH MY SPECIAL STUFFING

Roast turkey with all the trimmings is a 'must' for most families on Christmas Day, and it certainly is for mine. My turkey stuffing is not a traditional one, but I'm sure you'll agree it's a real winner with my Whisky Peppercorn Gravy, or you may prefer a traditional gravy, made with the juices in the pan your turkey has been cooked in.

Ingredients:
ROAST TURKEY (a 4.5kg-5.6kg (10lb-12lb) bird serves 10-12

A turkey needs cooking for about 15-20 minutes per 450g (1lb). Choose a turkey size according to the number of family or guests you will be serving. Preheat oven 190C, 375F, Gas Mark 5 (fan oven 170C). Clean and wash turkey inside and out, and pat thoroughly. I know it's traditional to stuff your turkey, but I usually put a large peeled onion inside the cavity, it keeps the flesh moist and enhances the flavour of the bird. Smear butter fairly thickly over the breast of the turkey, and sprinkle over some lemon zest mixed with crushed peppercorns. Secure its neck with a skewer and tie up the legs. Grease a large roasting tin and put the turkey in, covering it loosely with foil. Roast in preheated oven for 3-3½ hours (see times given above, depending on the size of your turkey). Test with a skewer into the thickest part of turkey thigh, if the juices run clear it's cooked, if they are pink, cook for a further 20 minutes and test again. Remove onion from bird and drain fat from tin, reserving enough pan juices to make your gravy, adding a little red wine or Madeira for flavour.

MY SPECIAL TURKEY STUFFING

Ingredients:

450g (1lb) minced pork
1 large tin chestnuts, chopped
2 celery sticks, chopped
1 garlic clove, crushed
Grated rind of 1 lemon
3 medium eggs
Salt & pepper to taste

4 chicken livers, chopped
110g (4oz) fresh brown breadcrumbs
1 onion grated
25g (1oz) butter
4 tablespoons chopped parsley
4-5 tablespoons brandy

Heat butter in frying pan and fry chicken livers. Then mix with all the other ingredients, stir in the brandy and eggs and season well. Stuff turkey in the usual way, or make into small balls and place around the turkey, or a separate dish, to cook for the last 25 minutes of the turkey's cooking time.

THYME AND PARSLEY STUFFING

If you prefer a more traditional stuffing, then try this one.

Ingredients:

110g (4oz) fresh white breadcrumbs
1 tablespoon chopped parsley
Salt & pepper to taste
1 egg, beaten

1 large onion, peeled & chopped
1 teaspoon thyme (or sage)
25g (1oz) dripping
110g (4oz) sausage meat

Mix all the ingredients together, but if you decide to make sage and onion stuffing, you will need to leave out the parsley, thyme and sausage meat, just add an extra teaspoon of chopped sage to the breadcrumbs. Stuff the bird or make into small round balls and cook separately in a little dripping for about 25 minutes.

WHISKY AND PEPPERCORN GRAVY

Gravy makes a meal, how many times have I heard that said! Well this one certainly does, and you will see from the quantities given in this recipe that you will have plenty left over to reheat the next day.

Ingredients:

Giblets from turkey
1 onion, peeled & chopped
Small wine glass whisky
150ml (¼ pint) single cream

2 litres (3½ pints) water
1 carrot, peeled & chopped
25g (1oz) flour
Few peppercorns & bunch of mixed herbs

Place giblets in a large pan, add water, onion, carrot, peppercorns and herbs. Bring to the boil, then simmer for one hour. Skim off scum that rises to the surface. You should end up with about 600ml-850ml (1-1½ pints) of stock. Use tin that your turkey has been cooked in, straining off the fat, and pour in the whisky and stir. Boil for 2 minutes and stir in the flour. Gradually add the strained stock, stirring well. Then pour in the cream, stirring to give a smooth gravy. Strain into a gravy boat.

CHEESY BITES

If you're having a party, try serving these tasty morsels, or with drinks when unexpected friends call in.

Ingredients:

110g (4oz) margarine
75g (3oz) tasty Cheddar cheese
¾ teaspoon salt
Pinch of chilli powder
Sesame seeds

2 tablespoons grated Parmesan cheese
110g (4oz) plain flour
½ teaspoon ground cumin
1 beaten egg

Blend margarine, Cheddar and Parmesan cheese in a food processor or by hand in a bowl with a large fork. Sift flour, salt, ground cumin and chilli powder and sprinkle over cheese mixture. Work together quickly, then use your hands to knead until a smooth round ball is formed. Wrap in a plastic bag and chill for about 30 minutes. Roll out on a floured surface into about 5mm (¼ inch) thickness, cut into triangles or fingers, then place bites on a lined baking tray and chill for 30 minutes. Brush lightly with beaten egg, sprinkle with sesame seeds and bake in preheated oven 180C, 350F, Gas Mark 4 for about 20 minutes until crisp and golden. Cool on tray and store in an airtight container.

TASTY SAUSAGE ROLLS

I make these sausage rolls with shortcrust pastry instead of flaky, and find they taste just as good and are very popular at Christmas time.

Makes about 24.

Ingredients:	Filling:
225g (8oz) self-raising flour	450g (1lb) sausage meat
150g (5oz) margarine & lard mixed	2 teaspoons finely chopped onion
1 tablespoon water	A little marmite stock

Make shortcrust pastry and roll out to about 20.5cm x 25.5cm (8 inches x 10 inches) and cut into two pieces. Mix sausage meat with chopped onion and moisten with stock. Make two long sausages of meat mixture and place each roll on right-hand side of each piece of pastry. Fold over left-hand side and press damp edges together. Cut into required sausage roll size to make approximately 24, beginning in the middle, score diagonally. Place on an ungreased baking tray, brush with milk or beaten egg and bake in preheated oven 200C, 400F, Gas Mark 6 for 25-30 minutes.

SWISS PIZZA

Another useful recipe to make at Christmas time, and if you have the time it's a good idea to make several and freeze them until needed; the pizza can be eaten hot or cold. You can also vary the topping according to your taste. To make a more robust pizza, try using wholemeal flour instead of the more traditional kind.

Serves 10.

Ingredients:	Filling:
225g (8oz) self-raising flour	450g (1lb) Emmenthal cheese
50g (2oz) lard	1 med onion, peeled & thickly sliced
50g (2oz) butter	Tomatoes and anchovy fillets
4 tablespoons very cold milk	
Pinch of salt	

Make pastry in the usual way and line a 15cm-20.5cm (6 inch x 8 inch) greased, shallow, fireproof baking dish with the pastry and prick it well. Add cheese, grated, and cover with a layer of thick slices of onion, then a layer of tomatoes. Finally top with crossed anchovy fillets to form a lattice pattern. Bake in preheated oven 200C, 400F, Gas Mark 6 for 30-40 minutes. Serve hot or cold.

VANILLA CREAM FLAN

An unusual creamy filling, which makes an attractive dessert to serve at a special dinner party, when your guests will probably ask for seconds, and you'll wish you had made a larger flan!

Serves 6.

Ingredients:

225g (8oz) ready-made
   shortcrust pastry
½ cup caster sugar
Pinch of salt
300ml (½ pint) milk, scalded
150ml (¼ pint) double cream

½ cup plain flour
6 egg yolks
425ml (¾ pint) lager
1 teaspoon vanilla essence
Grated chocolate to decorate

Roll out the shortcrust pastry and line a 20.5cm-23cm (8 inch-9inch) flan tin and bake blind. Beat egg yolks and mix with flour, sugar and salt in a saucepan over a very low heat, gradually stirring in the lager and milk. When thick, add vanilla and leave to cool. Whip cream and fold into mixture. Turn into flan case and decorate with grated chocolate. Serve chilled.

SPECIAL SUNDAY TRIFLE

It's traditional to make a trifle at Christmas time, and I usually have one ready in my fridge for family or guests, and even after Christmas lunch almost everyone can manage to eat a helping for tea – but do make the real custard – see my recipe for it in the November chapter.

Serves 6-8.

Ingredients:

175g (6oz) sponge cake
   (or 6 trifle sponges)
3 level tablespoons raspberry jam
4 tablespoons sherry
   (or use fruit juice)
1 x 200g (7oz) tin of raspberries

For the custard:

3 egg yolks
3 level tablespoons caster sugar
2 level tablespoons plain flour
425ml (¾ pint) milk
300ml (½ pint) whipping cream
6 ratafia biscuits
3 glacé cherries, halved
1 piece angelica, cut into 6
   diamond shapes

Cut sponge in half and sandwich it with raspberry jam, then place it in the base of a dish. Sprinkle over the sherry, and spoon over the raspberries and their juice.
To make custard: Beat the egg yolks, sugar and flour together, adding a little cold milk to moisten. Meanwhile, heat the remaining milk until boiling, and then pour it over the mixture, stirring constantly. Pour the custard back into the pan and bring to the boil, stirring all the time. Boil for one minute to cook the flour, remove from the heat and allow to cool slightly, and then pour it over the raspberries. Leave in a cool place to set. Whip up the cream until it holds its shape and spread it over the trifle. Decorate with the ratafia biscuits, cherries and angelica.

APRICOT SNOW

Dried fruits really come into their own during the winter months, and dried apricots are so versatile in puddings and light desserts like this one. I often serve this dessert at Christmas time, which I find aids the digestive system after the heavy meals and rich food most of us will have eaten during the festive season.

Serves 4.

Ingredients:

225g (8oz) dried apricots
2 tablespoons sugar
Icing sugar

4 egg whites
Vanilla essence
Fresh cream to serve

Wash apricots and put into a baking dish with enough water to cover. Soak for several hours. Put the dish in a preheated oven 180C, 350F, Gas Mark 4 and cook until soft (about ¾ hour). Drain the fruit and put through a sieve or purée in a liquidiser. Add the sugar and a few drops of vanilla essence. When cold fold in the stiffly beaten egg whites. Spoon into your prettiest glass serving dish, and sprinkle with icing sugar. Serve chilled with fresh whipped cream.

APPLE JELLY MOULD

A light, fruity dessert, which looks attractive when set out on a buffet table for a supper party over the festive season.

Serves 4.

Ingredients:

1 packet lemon jelly
Juice and grated rind of 1 lemon
2 eating apples, coarsely grated
Glacé cherries

300ml (½ pint) water
150ml (¼ pint) double cream, whipped
Whipped cream to decorate

Dissolve the jelly in water, add lemon juice and grated rind. Be sure to set a little jelly in the bottom of a mould. Stir the lightly whipped cream into the remaining jelly when it has reached the thick and syrupy stage. Now add the grated apple and pour into a mould when the first layer of jelly has set. Turn out when set firm and decorate with whipped cream and glacé cherries.

MY CHRISTMAS CAKE

Rich fruit cakes are best made at least six weeks before they are needed, but I usually make my Christmas cake about a month before, but it's not the end of the world if you make it later and marzipan and ice it in one 'go'. I don't always use the same recipe, but have used this one for the last few years.

Ingredients:

225g (8oz) butter
225g (8oz) dark brown sugar
5 eggs
110g (4oz) glace cherries
225g (8oz) plain flour
50g (2oz) ground almonds
1 teaspoon ground ginger
225g (8oz) currants

225g (8oz) sultanas
110g (4oz) raisins
110g (4oz) candied peel
½ teaspoon ground allspice
½ teaspoon ground cinnamon
½ teaspoon ground cloves
½ teaspoon ground coriander
½ gill brandy or whisky

Cream butter and sugar until light and soft. Gradually beat in the eggs and flour alternately. Lastly add the fruit and spices. Add a little of the spirits. Put into a greased and lined 20.5cm (8 inch) round cake tin and bake in preheated oven 170C, 325F, Gas Mark 3 for approximately 3 hours. When the cake is baked and while it is still hot it should be basted with the remaining spirits.

THE ALMOND PASTE

I must admit I do buy ready-made almond paste these days, I find it just as good as homemade if you buy a good quality paste, but for those of you who want to make your own, here is my recipe.

Ingredients to cover a 20.5cm (8 inch) cake:

225g (8oz) ground almonds
110g (4oz) icing sugar, sieved
A little almond and vanilla essence

110g (4oz) caster sugar
1 dessertspoon sherry
Egg to bind

Mix the ground almonds and the two sugars together. Add the flavourings and mix to a stiff paste with lightly beaten egg.

NB. You can use the yolk of the egg to make the almond paste, and use the remaining egg white to make your royal icing.

TO ALMOND PASTE THE TOP OF YOUR CAKE

Your cake should be perfectly level on top, and it's worth cutting a little away to correct any unevenness. Dust working surface with sugar. Knead and roll the paste to the exact size of the cake. Brush with beaten egg and invert the cake on to the icing. Press firmly together and neaten the edge with a knife, keeping the cake level. Turn the cake right side up and decorate or ice as desired.

ROYAL ICING

This icing is easy to make, and is excellent for piping as well as coating your cake. For a traditional and simple decoration you can roughen the icing up to make it look like a snow scene, and then add your decorations.

Ingredients:
350g (12oz) icing sugar
Sufficient white of an egg to make a stiff icing
Squeeze of lemon juice

Sieve the icing sugar. Put it into a large mixing bowl, add the lemon juice and sufficient lightly beaten egg white to give a stiff mixture. Beat thoroughly and use as required.

NB. While you are icing your cake it's a good idea to keep the bowl of mixture covered with a damp cloth, otherwise the icing begins to set on the surface and this can cause lumpiness.

APRICOT AND RASPBERRY SHORTIES

These fruity shorties are crisp and buttery to eat for tea or with your mid-morning cup of coffee, and stored in an airtight tin they will keep for a week.

Makes about 12-15.

Ingredients:

225g (8oz) self-raising flour	110g (4oz) butter
1 egg	50g (2oz) fine semolina
150g (5oz) caster sugar	A little vanilla essence

Sift flour, semolina and sugar together. Rub in butter with fingertips until it resembles fine breadcrumbs. Add vanilla essence and egg together to bind mixture. Mix well and then divide into 24 small balls, the size of a walnut. Flatten slightly and put into small, greased bun tins, make a dent in the middle of each bun and bake in a preheated oven 180C, 350F, Gas Mark 4 until golden brown. Cool slightly, then remove to a wire tray to cool. When completely cold, put raspberry jam in 12 of the buns and apricot jam in the remaining ones. Sprinkle a little icing sugar around the edges of each bun.

DORSET SPLITS

Spread with strawberry jam and cream these splits are really a slightly richer version of what we term as a scone. But whatever you prefer to call them, when cooked, they just cry out for a cup of tea to accompany them!

Makes about 14-15.

Ingredients:

225g (8oz) self-raising flour	¼ teaspoon salt
½ teaspoon mixed spice (optional)	75g (3oz) butter
75g (3oz) caster sugar	1 medium egg
Milk as required	

Sift flour, salt and spice into a mixing bowl. Rub in butter and mix to a stiff dough with the beaten egg and milk as required. Roll out to 1cm (½ inch) thickness. Cut into rounds, approximately 6cm (2½ inches). Place the splits on a greased baking tray, a little apart, and bake on shelf above the middle shelf of preheated oven 230C, 450F, Gas Mark 8 for about 12 minutes, until risen and golden brown. Cool on wire tray, and then split in two, spread half of each with strawberry jam, then cover with whipped cream and pair together.

SPICY CAKE WITH FUDGE ICING

This cake makes an attractive birthday cake for children, the fudge icing can be decorated for a special party occasion, and the cake freezes well, but omit the fudge icing until the cake is defrosted and needed.

Ingredients:
225g (8oz) butter
225g (8oz) soft brown sugar
4 eggs
225g (8oz) self-raising flour
50g (2oz) ground almonds
¾ teaspoon ground cloves
½ ground cinnamon

Fudge icing:
1 small tin evaporated milk
225g (8oz) granulated sugar
50g (2oz) butter or margarine
Vanilla essence

Cream butter and sugar together until light and fluffy. Gradually beat in the lightly whisked eggs and then add all the dry ingredients. Turn the mixture into a prepared 20.5cm (8 inch) greased and lined cake tin, and bake in preheated oven 180C, 350F, Gas Mark 4 for 1¾ hours. Or until cake is risen and golden brown. Cool on wire tray and top with fudge icing when completely cold.
To make the Fudge Icing: Put milk, butter and sugar into a heavy based saucepan and stir over a gentle heat until the sugar is dissolved. Then simmer gently until a rich golden colour, and test in a little cold water to see that the mixture turns into a soft icing. Remove from the heat, add vanilla essence and beat until it thickens. Pour quickly over the top of cake, and use a knife to swirl attractively over the topping. It's a good tip to leave the greaseproof paper around the cake while you are icing it.

MINCE PIES

I like my pastry to be thin and crisp, and I nearly always make shortcrust pastry as I find puff pastry too rich for these pies, especially if you want to top with a mixture of cream cheese and sugar as I've suggested in this recipe.

Makes 20-24

Ingredients:
300g (10½oz) plain flour
175g (6oz) butter
75g (3oz) caster sugar
Grated rind of half an orange
1 egg yolk and 3 tablespoons milk
1 tablespoon ground rice or
　ground almonds

For the filling:
400g (14oz) jar of mincemeat
　(preferably homemade)
2 tablespoons brandy
Icing sugar to dust

In a large mixing bowl mix the flour and ground rice, or almonds, add the butter in small pieces, and rub into mixture until it resembles fine breadcrumbs. Stir in the sugar, orange rind, egg and milk and mix to a dough. On a lightly floured surface knead to a smooth dough, then cover and chill for at least 30 minutes. Roll out very thinly and cut out 24 tops and bottoms with a 5cm (2 inch) pastry cutter, or a 6cm (2½) for less pies, to line tart tins. Stir brandy into mincemeat and spoon 1 medium teaspoon into each tart, but do not overfill the tart. Dampen the edges with water and seal the tops, and make a slit in each one. Bake in preheated oven 200C, 400F, Gas Mark 6 for 15-20 minutes until golden brown and dust with icing sugar. For a luxurious touch you can mix together about 175g (6oz) cream cheese and 60g (2½oz) caster sugar and put a teaspoon of this mixture on top of the mincemeat, then seal with the pastry lid. Delicious!

QUICK MINCEMEAT

Some cooks like to make their mincemeat well before December to let it mature, but I make mine a week before Christmas Day arrives, I find it keeps nice and moist and doesn't dry out so much.

Yields about 2¼ kg-2½ kg (5lb-5½lb)

Ingredients:

225g (8oz) raisins	175g (6oz) mixed peel
350g 12oz) sultanas	350g (12oz) currants
110g (4oz) suet	450g (1lb) soft dark brown sugar
2 teaspoons mixed spice	½ level teaspoon ground cinnamon
1 teaspoon ground nutmeg	6 tablespoons rum or sherry
700g (1½lb) peeled & cored	Grated rind & juice of 1 lemon &
cooking apples	1 orange

Mix together dried fruit and apples, then add the sugar, suet and spices and mix thoroughly. Finally, add grated rinds, juice and sherry or rum. Pot into jars and cover – what could be simpler!

Imperial/Metric Equivalents

VOLUME

1¼ml	¼tsp	
2½ml	½tsp	
5ml	1 level tsp	
15ml	1 level tbsp	
30ml	1 fl oz	
50ml	2 fl oz	
150ml	5 fl oz	¼ pint
200ml	7 fl oz	⅓ pint
300ml	10 fl oz	½ pint
425ml	15 fl oz	¾ pint
600ml	20 fl oz	1 pint
700ml		1¼ pints
850ml		1½ pints
1 litre		1¾ pints
1½litres		2 pints
2 litres		3½ pints

WEIGHT

10g	½oz
20g	¾oz
25g	1oz
50g	2oz
75g	3oz
110g	4oz
150g	5oz
175g	6oz
200g	7oz
225g	8oz
250g	9oz
275g	9½oz
300g	10½oz
350g	12oz
375g	13oz
400g	14oz
425g	15oz
450g	1lb
700g	1½lb
750g	1lb 10oz
1kg	2¼lb
1¼kg	2lb 12oz
1½kg	3lb 5oz
2kg	4½lb
2¼kg	5lb
2½kg	5lb 8oz
3kg	6lb 8oz

MEASUREMENT

3mm	⅛in
5mm	¼in
1cm	½in
2cm	¾in
2.5cm	1in
3cm	1¼in
4cm	1½in
5cm	2in
6cm	2½in
7.5cm	2¾in
9cm	3½in
10cm	4in
11.5cm	4½in
12.5cm	5in
15cm	6in
17cm	6½in
18cm	7in
20.5cm	8in
23cm	9in
24cm	9½in
25.5	10in
30.5cm	12in

AMERICAN CUP MEASURES

Butter, margarine, lard

25g	2 tbsp	¼ stick
100g	8 tbsp	1 stick

Breadcrumbs

Fresh 50g	1 cup
Dried 115g	1 cup

Cheese

Grated cheddar 115g	1 cup
Dice cheddar 170g	1 cup
Parmesan 150g	1 cup
Cream cheese 225g	1 cup

Dried Fruit

Currants, sultanas 150g	1 cup
Apricots 150-175g	1 cup
Prunes 175g	1 cup
Glace cherries 125g	1 cup

Fish

Prawns, peeled 175g	1 cup
Cooked and flaked 225g	1 cup

Flour

Cornflour 25g	¼ cup
Firmly packed flour 115g	1 cup

Liquids

Syrup, treacle, honey 350g	1 cup
Liquids 225ml	1 cup

Meat

Meat, minced & packed 225g	1 cup

Nuts

Almonds, whole/shelled 150g	1 cup
Almonds, flaked 115g	1 cup
Grounds nuts 115g	1 cup
Hazelnuts 150g	1 cup
Walnuts and pecans 115g	1 cup
Chopped nuts 115g	1 cup

Oats

Rolled oats 100g	1 cup
Oatmeal 175g	1 cup

Pulses

Split peas, lentils 225g	1 cup
Haricot beans 200g	1 cup
Kidney beans 300g	1 cup

Rice

Uncooked 200g	1 cup
Cooked and drained 165g	1 cup
Semolina, ground rice and couscous 175g	1 cup

Sugar

Caster & granulated 225g	1 cup
Moist brown 200g	1 cup
Icing sugar 125g	1 cup

Vegetables

Onions, chopped 115g	1 cup
Cabbage, shredded 75g	1 cup
Peas, shelled 150g	1 cup
Beansprouts 50g	1 cup
Potatoes, peeled & diced 170g	1 cup
Potatoes, mashed 225g	1 cup
Spinach, cooked puree 200-225g	1 cup
Tomatoes 225g	1 cup

MAXIMUM REFRIGERATOR STORAGE TIMES

The correct working temperature for a fridge is less than 5°C.

Raw meats

Joints	3 days
Poultry	2 days
Raw sliced meat	2 days
Minced meat	1 day
Offal	1 day
Sausages	3 days
Bacon	7 days
Raw fish	1 day

Cooked meats

Joints	3 days
Casseroles	2 days
Sliced meat	2 days
Ham	2 days
Cooked fish	1 day

Dairy foods

Milk	4-5 days
Cheese, soft	2-3 days
Cheese, hard	7-14 days
Eggs, raw	2 wks
Eggs, hard boiled	2 days
Freshly squeezed fruit juice	1 day
Cooked vegetables	2 days
Cooked potatoes	2 days

Canned foods	2 days*

*Once opened, canned foods should be transferred to a clean, dry container with a lid.

THAWING TIMES

At room temperature.

Meat

Joints over 1.5kg (3.3lb)	2-3 hrs
Cooked and flaked 225g	1-2 hrs

Poultry

All birds (min 9hrs) per 450g	3½ hrs

Vegetables

Cook from frozen

FREEZER STORAGE

Meat and poultry

Sausage & sausage meat	2-3mths
Minced beef	3-4mths
Offal	3-4mths
Ham and bacon joints	3-4mths
Beef, lamb, pork and veal	4-6mths
Duck, goose & rabbit	4-6mths
Chicken, turkey & venison	10-12mths

Fish

Shellfish	2-3mths

Oily fish	3-4mths
White fish	6-8mths

Fruit & Vegetables

Fruit juice	4-6mths
Mushrooms & tomatoes	6-8mths
Vegetables purees	6-8mths
Fruit	8-10mths
Most vegetables	10-12mths

Dairy produce

Cream	6-8mths
Butter, unsalted	6-8mths
Butter, salted	3-4mths
Cheese, hard	4-6mths
Cheese, soft	3-4mths
Ice cream	3-4mths
Milk, skimmed	3-4mths
Milk, semi-skimmed	3-4mths

Ready-prepared meals

Ready-prepared meals	4-6mths
Highly seasoned	2-3mths
Cakes	4-6mths
Bread	2-3mths
Bread dough	2-3mths

Guidelines for refrigerator and freezer storage and thawing times were provided by the Food Safety Advisory Centre. For further information contact Nicola on 020 7808 7256. Volume and weight values are inline with the British Weights & Measures Association.

OVEN TEMPERATURES

Celsius	Fahrenheit	Gas	Description
110°C	225°C	mark ¼	cool
130°C	250°C	mark ½	cool
140°C	275°C	mark 1	very low
150°C	300°C	mark 2	very low
170°C	325°C	mark 3	low
180°C	350°C	mark 4	moderate
190°C	375°C	mark 5	moderately hot
200°C	400°C	mark 6	hot
220°C	425°C	mark 7	hot
230°C	450°C	mark 8	very hot

For fan-assisted ovens reduce temperatures 10°C

ROASTING TIMES FOR MEAT AND POULTRY

Use these times as a guide but always check that pork and poultry are cooked through.

Beef		
Rare	20 mins per 450g (1lb) plus 20 mins	180°C (350°F)
Medium	25 mins per 450g (1lb) plus 25 mins	180°C (350°F)
Well done	30 mins per 450g (1lb) plus 30 mins	180°C (350°F)
Pork		
Medium	30 mins per 450g (1lb) plus 30 mins	180°C (350°F)
Well done	35 mins per 450g (1lb) plus 35 mins	180°C (350°F)
Lamb		
Medium	25 mins per 450g (1lb) plus 25 mins	180°C (350°F)
Well done	30 mins per 450g (1lb) plus 30 mins	180°C (350°F)
Poultry		
Well done	18 mins per 450g (1lb) plus 30 mins	190°C (375°F)

*Smaller joints weighing less than 1.25kg (2lb 12oz) may require 5 mins per 450g (1lb) extra cooking time.

Useful conversion chart – i.e. cooking by an Aga, electricity or gas

If you cook by an Aga or, like me, you cook by an electric cooker as well, these are the guidelines you should use when converting from cooking by electricity to cooking by an Aga.

Roasting Oven (Top Half)	400F-425F	200C-220C	*Gas Mark 6-7*
Roasting Oven (Lower Half)	350F-375F	180C-190C	*Gas Mark 4-5*
Baking Oven (Top Half)	325F-350F	170C-180C	*Gas Mark Low-Moderate*
Baking Oven (Lower Half)	225F-250F	110C-130C	*Gas Mark ¼-½*
Simmering Oven	225F-110C	*Gas ¼ Cool*	

I find if I am roasting a joint or chicken, weight 2kg (4½lb), in my Two-Oven Aga, it's best to put the meat, smeared with a little oil or butter and covered with foil, in the roasting oven, bottom half, for approximately 1 hour 40 minutes, and finish cooking with foil removed for the last 15 minutes of cooking time. To make sure the meat is cooked, test with a skewer and if the juices run clear, then it's cooked, but if they run pink then it isn't. You can always leave your joint or chicken in the oven a bit longer if you want to crisp the meat up more.

Remember to use your cold shelf as directed in your Aga Book. This shelf should be kept outside your Aga, but I must admit I always seem to keep mine in the simmering oven, and so far I haven't noticed any problems with my baking when I've used it in the roasting oven. *Good luck with your cooking what ever method you use!*

Seasons – Fruits and Vegetables

WHEN *FRUITS* ARE IN SEASON

This is to show when British-grown fruit is available.

	Jan	Feb	Mar	Apr	May	June	July	Aug	Sept	Oct	Nov	Dec
Apples –												
Cooking	•		•	•	•	•			•	•	•	•
Dessert	•	•	•							•	•	•
Blackberries									•	•		
Black/redcurrants						•	•	•				
Crab apples									•	•		
Cherries						•	•	•				
Chestnuts										•	•	•
Damsons								•	•	•		
Elderberries									•	•		
Gooseberries						•	•	•				
Greengages							•	•				
Loganberries							•	•				
Medlars										•	•	
Mulberries							•	•				
Pears	•	•	•					•	•	•	•	•
Plums						•	•	•	•	•		
Quinces										•	•	
Raspberries						•	•	•	•			
Rhubarb			•	•	•	•						
Strawberries					•	•	•	•	•	•		

169

WHEN *VEGETABLES* ARE IN SEASON

This is to show when British-grown vegetables are available.

	Jan	Feb	Mar	Apr	May	June	July	Aug	Sept	Oct	Nov	Dec
Artichokes –												
Globe						•	•	•	•			
Jerusalem	•	•	•	•						•	•	•
Asparagus					•	•						
Beans –												
Broad						•	•					
Runner							•	•	•	•		
Kidney						•	•	•	•			
Beetroot	•	•	•	•	•	•	•	•	•	•	•	•
Broccoli –												
Calabrese						•	•	•	•	•		
Sprouting			•	•	•							
Brussels –												
Top	•									•	•	•
Sprouts	•	•	•	•						•	•	•
Cabbage –												
January King	•	•	•	•						•	•	•
Drum Head								•	•	•	•	
Spring Green	•	•	•								•	•
Red	•	•										•
Carrot	•	•	•	•	•	•	•	•	•	•	•	•
Cauliflower	•	•	•	•	•	•	•	•	•	•	•	•
Celeriac	•	•	•							•	•	•
Celery				•	•	•	•	•	•	•	•	•
Chicory	•	•								•	•	•
Chinese Leaves			•	•	•	•	•	•	•	•		
Courgettes						•	•	•	•	•		
Cucumbers			•	•	•	•	•	•	•			
Endive				•	•	•	•					
Kale	•	•	•	•	•						•	•

	Jan	Feb	Mar	Apr	May	June	July	Aug	Sept	Oct	Nov	Dec
Leeks	•	•	•	•				•	•	•	•	•
Lettuce	•	•	•	•	•	•	•	•	•	•	•	•
Marrows						•	•	•	•	•		
Mint				•	•	•	•	•	•	•		
Mushrooms	•	•	•	•	•	•	•	•	•	•	•	•
Mustard and Cress	•	•	•	•	•	•	•	•	•	•	•	•
Onions	•								•	•	•	•
Parsley				•	•	•	•	•	•	•		
Parsnips	•	•	•	•					•	•	•	•
Peppers						•	•	•	•	•		
Peas					•	•	•	•	•	•		
Potatoes – New						•	•	•				
Maincrop	•	•	•	•	•				•	•	•	•
Pumpkin								•	•	•		
Radishes				•	•	•	•	•	•	•		
Seakale	•	•	•									•
Shallots	•								•	•	•	•
Spinach (best Mar/Apr)			•	•	•	•	•	•	•	•		
Spring onions				•	•	•	•	•				
Swedes	•	•	•	•	•				•	•	•	•
Sweetcorn								•	•	•		
Tomatoes					•	•	•	•	•	•		
Turnips	•	•	•			•	•	•	•	•	•	
Watercress	•	•	•	•	•	•	•	•	•	•	•	•

GLOSSARY OF COOKING TERMS

Acidulated water Water to which lemon juice or vinegar has been added in which fruit or vegetables, such as pears or Jerusalem artichokes, are immersed to prevent discolouration.

Agar-agar Obtained from various types of seaweed, this is a useful vegetarian alternative to gelatine.

Al dente Italian term used to describe food, especially pasta and vegetables, which are cooked until tender but still firm to the bite.

Arrowroot Fine, white powder used as a thickening agent for sauces. Unlike cornflour, it gives a clear gloss.

Au gratin Describes a dish which has been coated with sauce, then sprinkled with breadcrumbs or cheese and browned under the grill or in the oven.

Bain-marie Literally, a water bath, used to keep foods, such as delicate custards and sauces, at a constant low temperature during cooking. On the hob a double saucepan or bowl over a pan of simmering water is used: for oven cooking, the baking dish(es) is placed in a roasting tin containing sufficient hot water to come halfway up the sides.

Baking blind Pre-baking a pastry case before filling. Pastry case is lined with greaseproof paper and weighted down with dried beans or ceramic baking beans.

Baking powder A raising agent consisting of an acid, usually cream of tartar and an alkali, such as bicarbonate of soda. This expands during baking making cakes and breads rise.

Balsamic vinegar Italian oak-aged vinegar, dark brown in colour and has superior sweet, mellow flavour.

Bard To cover breast of game birds or poultry, or lean meat with fat to prevent the meat from drying out during roasting.

Baste To spoon juices and melted fat over meat, poultry, game or vegetables during roasting to keep them moist.

Béchamel Classic French white sauce, used as basis for other sauces and savoury dishes.

Beurre manié Equal parts of flour and butter kneaded together to form a paste. Used for thickening soups, stews and casseroles. Whisked into the hot liquid a little at a time at the end of cooking.

Blanch To immerse food briefly in fast-boiling water loosens skins, such as peaches or tomatoes – removes bitterness, destroys enzymes and preserves the colour, flavour and texture of vegetables (especially prior to freezing).

Bouquet garni Small bunch of herbs – a mixture of parsley stems, thyme and a bay leaf – tied in muslin – used to flavour stocks, soups and stews.

Braise To cook meat, poultry, game or vegetables slowly in a small amount of liquid in pan or casserole with a tight-fitting lid. Food is usually first browned in oil or fat.

Brochette Food cooked on a skewer or spit.

Brûlée A French term, meaning 'burnt' and used to refer to a dish with a crisp coating of caramelised sugar.

172

Canapé Small appetiser, consisting of a pastry or bread base with savoury topping, served with drinks.

Candying Preserving fruit or peel by impregnating with sugar.

Caper Small bud of a Mediterranean flowering shrub, packed in brine. Small French capers in balsamic vinegar – considered to be the best.

Caramelise Heat sugar or sugar syrup slowly until it is brown in colour; forms a caramel.

Carbonade Rich stews or braise of meat which includes beer.

Charcuterie French term for cooked pork, including hams, sausages and terrines.

Chine Sever the rib bones from the backbone, close to spine. This is done to meat joints, such as loin of pork or lamb, makes them easier to carve into chops after cooking.

Clarify Remove sediment or impurities from a liquid. Stock is clarified by heating with egg white – butter is clarified by melting and skimming. Butter which is clarified will withstand a higher frying temperature.
TO CLARIFY BUTTER heat until melted and bubbling stops. Remove from heat and let stand until sediment has sunk to the bottom – gently pour off the fat, straining through muslin.

Coconut milk Used in curries and other ethnic dishes. Available in cans from larger supermarketsand ethnic stores. Alternatively, creamed coconut sold compressed in blocks, can be reconstituted to make coconut milk.

Compote Mixture of fresh or dried fruit stewed in sugar syrup. Can be served hot or cold.

Concassé Diced fresh ingredient, used as a garnish – the term is most often applied to skinned, seeded tomatoes.

Coulis A smooth fruit or vegetable purée, thinned if necessary to a pouring consistency.

Court bouillon Aromatic cooking liquid containing wine, vinegar or lemon juice, used for poaching delicate fish, poultry or vegetables.

Cream of tartar Also known as tartaric acid, this is a raising agent which is also an ingredient of baking powder and self-raising flour.

Crêpe French term for a pancake.

Crimp To decorate the edge of pie, tart, or shortbread by pinching it at regular intervals – gives a fluted effect.

Croquette Seasoned mixture of cooked potato, fish, meat and poultry, or vegetables, shaped into small rolls, coated with egg and breadcrumbs and shallow-fried.

Croûte Circle or other shaped piece of fried bread, used as a base for serving small game birds.

Croûtons Small pieces of fried or toasted bread, served with soups and salads.

Crudités Raw vegetables, cut into slices or sticks, served with a dipping sauce as an appetiser.

Crystallise Preserve fruit in sugar syrup.

Curds Part of milk which coagulates when natural fermentation takes place or when a curdling agent, such as rennet, is added.

Cure To preserve fish, meat or poultry by smoking, drying or salting.

Deglaze To heat stock, wine or other liquid with the cooking juices left in the pan after roasting or sautéing, scraping and stirring to dissolve the sediment on base of the pan.

Dégorge Draw out moisture from a food, eg salting aubergines to remove bitter juices.

Dredge Sprinkle food generously with flour, sugar, icing sugar etc.

Dust Sprinkle lightly with flour, cornflour, icing sugar.

Emulsion A mixture of two liquids which do not dissolve into one another – oil and vinegar. Vigorous shaking or heating will emulsify them, as for a vinaigrette.

En croûte Foot which is wrapped in pastry before cooking.

En papillote Food which is baked in a greaseproof paper or baking parchment parcel and served from the paper.

Escalope Thin slice of meat, such as pork, veal or turkey, cut from the top of the leg and pan-fried.

Extract Concentrated flavouring used in small quantities, eg yeast extract, vanilla extract.

Farce Another term for stuffing.

Fillet Term used to describe boned breasts of birds, boned sides of fish, the undercut of a loin of beef, lamb, port or veal etc.

Filo Pastry Type of Greek pastry manufactured in wafer-thin sheets and sold in packets or boxes.
Must be kept covered to prevent it drying out.

Fine herbes French mixture of chopped herbs, ie parsley, tarragon, chives and chervil.

Flambé Flavouring a dish with alcohol – brandy or rum, which is then ignited so that the actual alcohol content is burned off.

Frosting Coat leaves and flowers with a fine layer of sugar to use as a decoration. An American term for icing cakes.

Galette A cooked savoury or sweet mixture shaped into a round.

Garnish Decoration, usually edible, such as parsley or lemon, which is used to enhance the appearance of a savoury dish.

Gelatine An animal-derived gelling agent sold in powdered form, and as leaf gelatine. Used in jellies, mousses and cold soufflés.

Gelazone A vegetarian gelling agent sold in powdered form in sachets – used as a substitute for gelatine.

Ghee Clarified butter widely used in Indian cookery.

Glaze Glossy coating given to sweet and savoury dishes – improves their appearance and sometimes flavour. Ingredients for glazes include beaten egg, egg white, milk and syrup.

Gluten Protein constituent of grains, such as wheat and rye, which develops when the flour is mixed with water to give the dough elasticity.

Griddle Flat, heavy, metal plate used on the hob for cooking scones or for searing savoury ingredients.

Hors d'oeuvre Selection of cold foods served together as an appetiser.

Hull To remove the stalk and calyx from soft fruits, such as strawberries etc.

Infuse Immerse flavourings, such as aromatic vegetables, herbs, spices and vanilla, in a liquid to impart flavour. The infused liquid is brought to the boil, then left to stand for a while.

174

Julienne Fine 'matchstick' strips of vegetables or citrus zest, used as a garnish.

Knead To work dough by pummelling with the heel of the hand.

Knock back Knead a yeast dough for a second time after rising, to ensure an even texture.

Liaison Thickening or binding agent based on a combination of ingredients, such as flour and water, or oil and egg.

Macerate Soften and flavour raw or dried foods by soaking in a liquid, eg soaking fruit in alcohol.

Mandolin(e) Flat wooden, or metal frame with adjustable cutting blades for cutting vegetables.

Marinate To soak raw meat, poultry or game – in a mixture of oil, wine, vinegar and flavourings – to soften and impart flavour. The mixture, which is known as a marinade, can also be used to baste the food during cooking.

Medallion Small round piece of meat – beef or veal.

Mocha Term means a blend of chocolate and coffee.

Parboil Boil a vegetable or other food for part of its cooking time before finishing it by another method.

Pare Finely peel the skin or zest from vegetables or fruit.

Passata A purée of plum tomatoes, used in many Italian dishes. Ready-made from supermarkets.

Pâte French word for pastry, familiar in pâte sucrée, a sweet flan pastry.

Pâté Savoury mixture of finely chopped or minced meat, fish and/or vegetables, served as a starter with bread or toast and crudités.

Pectin A naturally occurring substance found in most varieties of fruit and some vegetables – necessary for setting jams and jellies. Commercial pectin and sugar with pectin are also available for preserve-making.

Pesto Paste-like sauce made from puréed herbs and oil, used to flavour pasta and vegetables. A classic pesto is made from basil, pine nuts, garlic and olive oil.

Pickle Preserve meat or vegetables in brine or vinegar.

Poach Cook food gently in liquid at simmering point, so that the surface of the liquid is just trembling.

Pot roast Cook meat in a covered pan with some fat and a little liquid.

Prove Leave bread dough to rise after shaping.

Purée Pound, sieve or liquidise fruit, vegetables or fish to a smooth pulp. Purées often form the basis for soups and sauces.

Quenelles Fish, meat or poultry blended to a fine paste and shaped into ovals, then poached in a liquid.

Reduce Fast-boil stock or other liquid in an uncovered pan to evaporate water and concentrate the flavour.

Refresh To cool hot vegetables quickly by plunging into ice-cold water or holding under running water – stops the cooking process and preserves the colour.

Render Melt fat slowly to a liquid, either by heating meat trimmings, or to release the fat from fatty meat, ie duck or goose, during roasting.

Rennet Animal-derived enzyme used to coagulate milk in cheese-making. Vegetarian alternative is available.

Roulade Soufflé or sponge mixture usually rolled around a savoury or sweet filling.

Roux Mixture of equal quantities of butter (or other fat) and flour cooked together to form the basis of many sauces.

Salsa Piquant sauce made from chopped fresh vegetables and fruit.

Sauté Cook food in a small quantity of fat over a high heat, shaking the pan constantly – in a sauté pan (a frying pan with straight sides and a wide base).

Scald Pour boiling water over food to clean it, or loosen skin, eg tomatoes. Also used to describe heating milk to just below boiling point.

Score Cut parallel lines in the surface of food to improve its appearance or help it cook more quickly.

Sear Brown meat quickly in a little hot fat before grilling or roasting.

Shred Grate cheese or slice vegetables into very fine pieces or strips.

Sieve Press food through a perforated sieve to obtain a smooth texture.

Simmer Keep a liquid just below boiling point.

Skim Remove froth, scum or fat from the surface of stock, gravy, stews, jam etc. Use a skimmer, a spoon or absorbent kitchen paper.

Smoke Cure meat, poultry and fish by exposure to wood smoke.

Spit Rotating rod on which meat, poultry or game is cooked – in an oven or over an open fire.

Souse Pickle food, fish etc. in vinegar flavoured with spices.

Steep Immerse food in warm or cold liquid to soften it, and sometimes to draw out strong flavours.

Sterilise Destroy bacteria in foods by heating.

Stew Cook food, such as tougher cuts of meat, slowly in flavoured liquid which is kept at simmering point.

Stir-fry To cook small even-sized pieces of food rapidly in a little fat, tossing constantly over a high heat, usually in a wok.

Sweat Cook chopped or sliced vegetables in a little fat without liquid in covered pan over a low heat.

Syrup, sugar Concentrated solution of sugar in water used to make sorbets, granitas, fruit juices etc.

Tepid Term used to describe temperature at approximately blood heat, ie 37°C (98.7°F).

Thermometer, Sugar/Fat Used for accurately checking temperature of boiling sugar syrups, and fat for deep-frying, respectively.

Unleavened Bread made without a raising agent.

Vanilla sugar Sugar in which a vanilla pod has been stored to impart its flavour.

Zest Thin coloured outer layer of citrus fruit which contains essential oil.

Zester Small bevelled tool with five holes drawn across citrus fruit to remove the zest in fine strips.